THE
LITTLE GIANT® BOOK
Dominoes

Jennifer A. Kelley & Miguel Lugo

Sterling Publishing Co., Inc.
NEW YORK

10 9 8 7 6 5 4 3 2 1

Published in 2003 by Sterling Publishing Co., Inc.
387 Park Avenue South, New York, N.Y. 10016
This edition is excerpted from *The Great Book of Domino Games* © 1999 by Jennifer A. Kelly and from *Competitive Dominoes* © 1998 by Miquel Lugo
© 2003 by Sterling Publishing Co., Inc.
Distributed in Canada by Sterling Publishing
c/o Canadian Manda Group, One Atlantic Avenue, Suite 105
Toronto, Ontario, Canada M6K 3E7
Distributed in Great Britain and Europe by
Chris Lloyd at Orca Book Services
Stanley House, Fleets Lane, Poole BH15 3AJ, England
Distributed in Australia by Capricorn Link (Australia) Pty. Ltd.
P.O. Box 704, Windsor, NSW 2756, Australia
Printed in China
All rights reserved

Sterling ISBN 1-4027-0290-6

CONTENTS

Foreword

Many adults enjoy playing with dominoes. Some like the competition; for others, it's simply a relaxing way to pass the time with friends. Children love to play dominoes, too. It's a great way for them to learn important math skills, because it makes learning interesting and fun. It also gives them an opportunity to develop good sportsmanship.

Domino games can provide hours of entertainment for the entire family. Most games are easy to learn and include elements of both skill and chance. Playing dominoes is a way to exercise your mind and a pleasurable, fun activity to enjoy with friends.

Whether you enjoy playing dominoes when you're by yourself or at a party with as many as eight or more players; whether you're very young, a beginner, or an experienced dominoes player, you'll find a wide assortment of games here to choose from.

All you need for most games is a set of dominoes and a flat playing surface, like a table or a board. Most domino sets are fairly inexpensive and will last a lifetime. So, what are you waiting for? Let's play!

A Small World

I have three American friends who come from different parts of the world: Moscow, Iraq (he's Kurdish), and Mexico City. They moved to the United States after living at least twenty years in other countries. Yet, in response to my questions about domino play in their native countries, they amazingly all essentially described to me the same basic game, "Block."

I say "amazingly" because, in researching domino game names and rules for this book, I found very many different variations to many different variations of variations! I searched out games from around the globe and organized them into categories, and subcategories! After going through hundreds of different domino games, and even hundreds more ways of playing those different domino games, I realized I was discovering the same domino games over and over again.

Getting back to my friends, the one from Moscow said the domino game he remembers is called "Kozel" in Russian, which translates to "Goat." My Kurdish friend told me about the tea shops in Iraq where men pass the time playing dominoes with friends, drinking tea, and just generally "hanging out." My friend from Mexico said the game there is nearly always played with partners. Perhaps one reason is that, in Mexico, communication between partners—the use of a special code-language to alert your partner that you hold a good hand, a bad hand, you don't hold the tile he or she needs, and so on—is considered a skill to be mastered. In the United States, on the other hand, any kind of such communication between partners in any form is considered cheating and, in tournament play, is absolutely not tolerated! Even small worlds do have their differences.

History of Domino Games

The actual origin of the game of dominoes—who invented the game and where and when it was first played—is unknown. There is evidence that a version of the basic matching game, where tiles are matched end to end, was played in the Far East in ancient times, but the basic game that we know today first appeared in Italy in the eighteenth century. From Italy, it seems to have spread to France and then was brought to England by prisoners of war about 1790. In 1801, Joseph Strutt, in his book *Sports and Pastimes of the People of England*, expressed his view of one of the most popular games of the period. The game simply went by the name "Dominoes," and he described it as "a very childish sport, imported from France a few years back."

Some attempts have been made to trace the entry of dominoes into Europe from the Far East, perhaps through the Middle East, but so far no clear-cut connection has been established. As far as can be determined by historical evidence, dominoes seem to have existed in the Far East long before they appeared in the West. This does not necessarily mean, however, that there is a direct connection. The relatively elementary concept of the basic matching game played with dominoes may well have evolved in Europe quite independently, especially in view of its possible connection with dice.

Dominoes—the pieces and the rules of play—are known throughout the Orient. Only the Chinese, however, have left us with much of a history, and a good part of that may be legendary.

According to some accounts, domino pieces can be traced to Hung Ming, a soldier-hero who lived from A.D. 181 to 234. Others attribute it to the ingenuity of Keung T'ai Kung in the 12th century

B.C. The *Chu sz yam*, "Investigations on the Traditions of All Things," states that domino pieces were invented in A.D. 1120 by a statesman who presented them to the Emperor Hui Tsung, and that they were circulated abroad by imperial order during the reign of Hui Tsung's son, Kao Tsung (A.D. 1127–1163). Other interpreters of this document, however, maintain that it refers not to the invention of domino pieces and a particular game played with those pieces but to the standardization of domino pieces and game rules; domipieces and games played with dominoes having been in existence long before that. All in all, there is no historical evidence which points conclusively to the invention of the first domino games. Most likely, as is the case with most games, the rules to the games evolved gradually rather than being a singular invention.

Mah-jongg, a game for four people which uses 144 pieces, originated in China and by 1400, it hadspread all over China. Some people consider mah-jongg to be the "great-grandfather" of dominoes. R.C. Bell, an English game researcher, believes that dominoes were clearly a Chinese invention. Others see Arabia as the country of origin. In Egypt, it's still one of the most popular café games.

Dominoes became popular in coffee houses during the nineteenth century, and in 1820 a book by C. van Greeven was published in Dutch at The Hague. It was entitled *The deceits that people commit at the so-called game of dominoes unmasked.*

Dominoes are not mentioned in *Hoyle's Games Improved* (1814). Even in the 1853 edition, *Hoyle's Games Improved and Enlarged*, the game merits only a page and a half, with the entry starting: "Domino is played by 2 to 4 persons with 28 pieces of oblong ivory, plain at the back, but in the face divided by a black line in the middle and indented with spots from one to a double-6." A lengthy description of the individual pieces then follows. In all the early pieces seen by the author, however, the "ivory" was bone. The account also contains the remark "Sometimes a double set is played with, of which double-12 is the highest." The game described is "The Block Game." Hoyle's short entry ends with this admonition: "This game requires strict attention, and nothing but practice will make perfect."

Origin of the Word "Domino"

The word domino was probably derived from the Latin word dominus, which means "the master of the house." The vocative domine became the Scottish and English dominic (schoolmaster), and the dative or ablative domino became the French, then the English, domino, which referred at first to a sort of monastic hood; then to a hooded masquerade costume with a small mask; then to the mask itself; and finally to one of the pieces in the game. It thus became dominoes, presumably from the fancied resemblance between a mask and one or more of the pieces, probably the 1-1. The word domino was accepted by the Académie Française in 1798 as the name of the game and the name of the pieces.

History of Domino Pieces

The ancients used sticks, stones, and bones as a way of adding. Perhaps, later, they may have used flat rocks, bones, or pieces of wood with dots to represent numbers counted. As man began to communicate verbally, he gave names to the numbers and developed a counting system as high as the number of fingers and toes he had. Thus, the objects used for tallying may have had dots up to 20.

As civilizations progressed, merchants used stacks of rocks for computing. Later, the Babylonians used clay tiles for counting. A stylus was used to press cuneiform numerals on the clay tiles. These tiles could have been used to keep a record of business transactions in banking or taxes. It takes only a minor stretch of the imagination to see the tiles being transformed into pieces with which to play games.

The Greeks and the Hindus used the 10-numeral (decimal) system for counting. About A.D. 500, a Hindu devised a positional notation for the numerals. The Hindus modernized the first nine symbols from 1 to 9. The zero came in use about A.D. 825, when an Arab mathematician of Baghdad recommended that Hindu numerals be used by merchants and mathematicians of both East and

West. With the development of the numerals from 1 to 9, objects similar to dominoes and dice were used in our counting system. After the zero was added, the 21-domino set got the blanks for a suit; thus our standard set of 28 dominoes was formed and used for games and counting in business.

By the thirteenth century, our humble objects of the numerals came to Italy from the trade conducted by long Arab caravans to India and China. Dominoes may have been introduced into the business of Europe at that time. In the fifteenth century, objects similar to dominoes were used to teach arithmetic at a private school in Mantua, Italy. The use of dominoes for games and objects of counting in trading and banking continued to develop in the cities of Venice, Florence, and Genoa.

The earliest dominoes were made of rectangles of bone with plain backs and pips drilled into the fronts. Many were made by French prisoners of war from mutton and beef bones and were sold to augment the prisoners' meager allowances. Others were the work of seamen, whiling away their leisure hours on long voyages. Some of these sets were novelty items, including then well-known "birdcage sets."

Suitable thick pieces of bone were scarce, necessitating the use of thinner pieces fastened onto an ebony backing with glue and a central brass sprig. Later, other hardwoods were stained to simulate ebony, and the central sprig was reinforced with two smaller sprigs.

In 1855, Charles Lepage of Paris invented *bois durci*, a substitute for wood, bone, metal, and other hard substances, consisting of rosewood or ebony sawdust and albumen from eggs and blood. The sawdust was soaked in pure albumen and water; the mixture was then dried and placed in a steel mold and subjected to heat and pressure in a hydraulic press. *Bois durci* domino sets, or even single pieces, are now rare and are desirable collectors' items.

Bois durci, the first plastic, was followed a year later by celluloid, originally known as Parkesine and now called Xylonite. This material was first made by Parkes of Birmingham in 1856 and used for dominoes, but unfortunately it was highly flammable. In the late nineteenth century, cheap domino sets were made of tinplate for use in public houses, and were often provided at nominal cost or even free by tobacco companies.

Bakelite appeared about 1910, named after Dr. Leo Baekeland, the inventor. Made from phenols and formaldehyde, this synthetic resin could be poured, cast and molded. Bakelite quickly came into popular use for carved jewelry. Dominoes were also made using the new material, as was important automobile electrical insulation. The Bakelite patent expired in 1927 and was acquired by Catalin Corporation. Bakelite-Catalin was used to make molded radio cases as well as carved jewelry and, of course, dominoes. Bakelite and Catalin became obsolete after World War II with the advent of injection and compression-molded plastics.

Colored sheets of Perspex, though expensive, can be used to make attractive dominoes that are pleasant to the touch. Black and white sheets of Perspex are cemented together then cut into rectangles and the pips are hand-drilled and painted.

Today, all mass-produced dominoes are made either of wood, urea compression molded plastic, or poured marblelike polyester resin. Wooden dominoes with designs impressed on their backs, largely made in South America, are inexpensive for children's toys. The most popular dominoes for adult games are made of urea plastic, from China, or marblelike resin by Puremco, a Texas company. Domino sets today are available in several colors, including ivory, and even specially personalized.

As for domino play, there's little difference around the world, and new games will undoubtedly be created in the years ahead, so whenever you travel and find a friendly game in progress, be an onlooker for a while, then join in and try your skill. Whatever its derivation, dominoes is a fantastic game. Our thanks for many entertaining hours should go to the unknowns who first invented the tiles and the game.

Introduction to Dominoes

The Pieces

Domino pieces are sometimes called tiles, rocks, blocks, stones, bones, men, or seeds.

Small, flat, rectangular-shaped game pieces made of plastic, wood, bone, ivory, stone, or other material, they are usually twice as long as they are wide. The tiles in most sets are made to be exactly half as thick as they are wide so that they can stand on edge without falling over. A domino may be of any size, but an ordinary domino is about one inch wide and two inches long.

Like a playing card, a domino has a *face* and a *back*. The back of each tile is either blank or the back of every tile in the set is decorated with an identical design. The face of each tile is divided by a line across the center separating the piece into two halves. Numbers are represented in each half by spots, commonly called *pips*, or the absence of spots, which represents zero. A half that doesn't have pips is called a zero, blank, pale, or white.

When dominoes are made, the pips are uniformly molded or drilled and then painted. The pips are usually black if the tile is white; white, if the tile is black. However, domino sets can be found in almost any color combination.

This domino face has 1 pip on one half and 6 pips on the other half and is called the 1-6 domino. Dominoes with the same number of pips on each half of the face are known as *doubles* or *doublets*. A *single* domino, also referred to as a *combination* domino, has a different number of pips on

A DOMINO FACE

each half of the face. All the tiles in a set of dominoes that have the same number of pips (or the absence of any) on one end make up a *suit*. For example, the 0-0, 0-1, 0-2, 0-3, 0-4, 0-5, and 0-6 pieces make up the suit of zero. Each double belongs to only one suit; singles belong to two suits. For example, the 1-6 belongs to the 1 suit and the 6 suit. Dominoes are also thought of as having *weights*. A domino is heavier than another domino if it has more pips. A domino is lighter if it has fewer pips.

In most domino games, the number of pips on a domino are added or subtracted for scoring purposes. In some domino games, however, the number of pips on a domino are used strictly for matching purposes. In these matching games, dominoes with pictures, colors, or shapes on each half of the domino face could be used just as easily as dominoes with pips. Many domino sets made for children have colorful pictures on the face of each domino instead of pips.

The Domino Set

A set of domino pieces is sometimes called a deck. The three most common domino sets are the double-6, double-9, and double-12 sets.

The set is named after the domino in the set with the highest number of pips. Most domino games are designed to be played with the double-6 set.

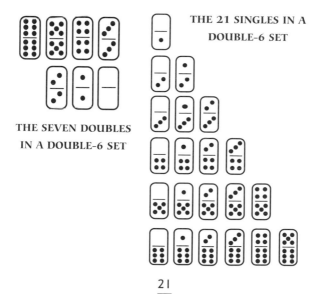

THE 21 SINGLES IN A DOUBLE-6 SET

THE SEVEN DOUBLES IN A DOUBLE-6 SET

Every set of dominoes includes all possible combinations of two numbers, from zero (blank) up to the highest number of pips in the set (for example, 12 in a double-12 set), as well as a double for each suit. Each combination of pips occurs only once in a set.

A standard double-6 domino set consists of 28 tiles: 7 doubles and 21 singles.

In a double-6 set, each number appears eight times: once each on six tiles and twice on the double tile. A double-9 set consists of 55 tiles, with each number appearing 11 times. A double-12 set consists of 91 tiles, with each number appearing 14 times. A double-15 set of tiles is the latest to hit the market—and with phenomenal success.

The Stock and Hands

The set of dominoes from which a player draws his hand before the game and the tiles remaining, which are drawn from throughout the game when necessary, is called the stock, the boneyard, the kitty, or the reserve.

Most domino games are played with *hands*. The unplayed tiles each player holds in his possession make up his hand. Before the game, each player picks tiles from the stock to make up his hand. In some domino games, it may be the rule to add more tiles to your hand throughout the game by picking them from the stock. Every time a player makes a play, a tile is subtracted from his hand and, when the game is over, the tiles left in the player's possession, if any, are also considered his hand. (The word "hand" also often refers to the series of plays from when the first domino is set to when a player "dominoes." A game of dominoes will comprise several such hands.)

Modifying

Many games can easily be modified for play with other sets, or vice versa. To modify a set, tiles from the double-6 set can be removed to create a double-5 set or a double-3 set, for example, if that is what you need to play. Or tiles from the double-12 set can be removed to create a double-10 set. Just make sure that your "created" set contains all the possible combinations of two numbers, from zero (blank) up to the highest number of pips in the set, as well as a double for each suit. Each combination of pips occurs only once in a set.

The obvious reason for modifying the rules to be played with a different set is that you don't have the set called for. There are, however, other reasons: (1) it can change the level of difficulty of the game; (2) it can accommodate more players or fewer players; and, (3) it can shorten or lengthen a game. So, you have lots of options to choose from.

Domino Terms

Ace The end of a tile with one pip.

Arm A row of dominoes set in a straight line in the layout of a matching or scoring game.

Bid The number of points a player in a bidding game anticipates making for that hand. The player winning the bid (highest bidder) earns the right to name the trumps and also to make the first play of the hand.

Block (1) In a matching or scoring game, the process of playing a domino which cannot be followed in suit by your opponent. (2) Domino pieces are sometimes called *blocks*. (3) Another name for the Block Game.

Blocked Game In a matching or scoring game, if (1) no player is able to make a play; (2) draw from the boneyard; and, (3) all players are still holding tiles in their hand, the game is said to be "blocked." At which time the game is over and is said to have "ended in block."

Blocking Games Games in which scoring is done only at the end of each hand and not after individual plays are made. Play is aimed at blocking your opponent and being the first player to play all the tiles in your hand.

Count Dominoes (1) In bidding games, the tiles that have pips that total 5 or a multiple of 5. If playing with one set of double-6 tiles, for example, the count dominoes would include the 5-5 and 6-4 (each worth 10 points) and the 5-0, 3-2, and 4-1 (each worth 5 points). (2) In scoring games, tiles played so that the sum of the pips on the exposed ends of the layout total 5 or a multiple of 5.

Cutthroat (1) Any domino game in which each player plays independently, for himself, without a partner. (2) A 3-handed game or any game with 4 or more players in which each player plays for himself, without a partner. (3) The name of a 4-handed, Texas-style game of dominoes, in which each player plays for himself, without a partner.

Deuce The end of a tile with two pips.

Domino (1) One of the pieces, or tiles, in a set of dominoes. (2) In matching and scoring games, to be the first player to play the last tile in his hand, and therefore, win that hand. **Dominoed** When a person is the first to play the last tile in his hand, he is said to have "dominoed." **Dominoer** The person playing the last remaining domino in his hand.

Go Out When a player is the first to play the last tile in his hand in a matching or scoring game.

Head Up A game of dominoes played by only two players.

Leader (1) The player who plays first, puts down the first tile. (2) In a matching or scoring game, a double tile played when the player has no matching dominoes in his hand.

Round Games (1) "Party games" for a large group of people. (2) Games in which each player plays for himself.

Scoring Games Games in which scores are made during play and at the end of the hand.

Set (1) In a bidding game, if a player cannot make his bid, he is said to be "set." (2) In matching and scoring games, the first tile played.

Spinner (1) A double in the layout which may be played on both sides and both ends. Matching and scoring games each have a rule about spinners: a) There are no spinners; b) Only the first double played is a spinner; or c) All doubles are spinners. (2) In games where only the first double played is a spinner, "spinner" refers to the first double played.

Suit(s) Dominoes having the same number of pips on one end. For example: the 0-6, 1-6, 2-6, etc., are all from the 6 suit.

Trey The end of a tile with three pips.

Trick A term used in bidding games. In the game of Forty-Two, for example, each of the four players plays 1 tile per trick. The trick is won by the player who played the winning tile of the 4 tiles played. There are 7 tricks in the game of Forty-Two.

Trumps (1) In bidding games, the winning bidder earns the opportunity to name trumps for that hand. The word "trump" comes from the word "triumph." A domino from the trump suit automatically "triumphs" over other dominoes played. (2) Doubles are sometimes referred to as "trumps."

Widow or Widows The tile, or tiles, left after each player has drawn hands from the deck at the beginning of a hand. Also called "the boneyard." However, the term "the boneyard" is typically used in matching and scoring games and usually refers to tiles that are purposely not drawn at the beginning of the game, so that players can draw from the boneyard during the game when they do not hold a playable tile in their hand. The term "widow(s)" is typically used in bidding games and usually refers to the tile or tiles left after all players have drawn their hands from the deck at the beginning of the hand and there are "widow(s)" because the number of tiles cannot be divided equally among the number of players.

Domino Rules: The Basics

You may already play some domino games. If so, you may find that the rules here are not exactly the same as those you have learned. Many domino games go by different names yet have extremely similar, sometimes even identical, rules. Also, many games go by the same name in various parts of the world, but the rules vary from place to place.

I have tried to make this book as complete as possible, including every variation to every game for which I was able to find rules. Whether you follow the rules precisely, or whichever variation of any game you choose to use, is irrelevant as long as all the players clearly understand what the rules of play are and agree to them before a game begins. It is also, of course, important to be sure the rules you choose to play by are functional. Even so, a situation may arise in play that is not covered by any rule in this book. In such a case, it may be necessary for the players to agree on a workable rule to cover the problem.

The basic rules in this chapter apply to most of the games in this book, but not all of them. For example, there are a few games included where hands are not drawn and, of course, the basic rules that pertain to more than one player would not apply to solitaire games.

In many domino games, as players make their plays, a line of tiles is formed on the table usually, but not always, by matching the pips on the open end of the domino. This formation of tiles is called the line of play. There are basic instructions liste-under "Line of Play" (page 39) specifically for those games.

Shuffling the Tiles

Before every game, a player shuffles the tiles face-down on a flat playing surface, thoroughly mixing them by moving them with his hands. The player's hands may not remain on the same tiles while shuffling, and the player doing the shuffling should be the last to draw his hand for the game.

Players may choose to take turns shuffling before each game or the same player may shuffle the dominoes before each game. Here are two of several options: (1) The player to the right of the player making the first play does the shuffling for a game; or (2) The winner of the previous game shuffles for the next game.

Seating Arrangement

A player's position at the table in a game with three or more players is called a *seat*.

One way to determine seating arrangements is by lot. After the tiles are shuffled, each player draws a domino from the stock. The player who draws the tile with the greatest number of pips (the heaviest tile) has the first choice of seating. The player holding the next highest seats himself to the left, and so on. If there is a tie, it is broken by drawing new dominoes from the stock. The tiles are returned to the stock and reshuffled before the players draw their hands. When a partnership game is played, the partners sit opposite each other.

Setting Order of Play

There are several different ways to determine which player will make the first play: You can draw lots, begin the game by setting the heaviest domino, or have the winner of the previous game make the first play of the next game. After it is determined who will make the first play of the game, the order of play will be decided by the seating arrangement. Play will continue to the left, clockwise, after the first play is made. Or, you may choose to play in a counterclockwise rotation, as is done in some Latin American countries, as long as all players agree to it before the game.

Drawing lots to determine first play: After the tiles are shuffled, each player draws a domino from the stock. The player who draws the heaviest tile will make the first play. If there is a tie, it is broken by drawing new dominoes from the stock.

Begin by selling heaviest domino: In some domino games, the rules state that the first play must be made by the player with the highest double in his hand. Rules for other games state that the first play must be made by the player with the heaviest domino, double or single, as the case may be.

If *highest double*, after the tiles are shuffled, each player draws his hand from the stock. The player who draws the highest double of the set (i.e., double-9 if playing with a double-9 set), plays·it as the lead. If the highest double was not drawn, the second-highest double is played. If the second-highest double was not drawn, the third-highest double is played, and so on, until a double is played. If none of the players holds a double in his hand, all hands are discarded, reshuffled, and new hands are drawn. After the first player sets his double, the second play is made by the player to his left and play continues clockwise.

If *heaviest tile*, follow the instructions above for highest double with this exception: Instead of drawing new hands if no player holds a double tile, the player holding the heaviest single begins play.

Winner of last game goes first: The winner of the last game played may open the next game. Or, if a game ends in a tie, the player who placed the last tile plays the first tile in the next game.

Drawing the Hand

Each player draws the number of tiles specified in the rules for the domino game being played and then positions them in front of himself in such a way that the other players cannot see the pips on his tiles.

After all hands have been drawn, there may be a surplus of tiles left in the stock. These tiles should remain facedown and, depending on the rules of the game being played, may be bought later in that game (see "Passing and Buying," page 38).

Opening the Game

Determine who will make the first play as explained above and according to the rules of the particular domino game being played. The player making the first play may be referred to as the setter, the downer, or the leader. He should place his tile faceup in the middle of the table.

The words *set*, *down*, and *lead* are all used as verbs to refer to the act of making the first play of the game. "The set," "the down," and "the lead" are used as nouns to refer to the first domino played in a game and also the first play of the game.

Here is a rule variation that players may agree to employ: Any time a player plays a double, whether for the opening of the game or during the play of the game, he may immediately play a *second* tile onto his double before the next player makes his play.

Passing and Buying

Any player who does not hold in his hand a tile with the correct number of pips, and therefore cannot make the next play, must either pass or buy from the stock, according to the rules of the game. Some games permit players to skip a play if they so choose, even if they hold a playable tile.

Passing is also called knocking or renouncing. A player unable to make a play must announce to the other players "I pass"; then the next player takes his turn. If no one is able to make a play, the game ends.

In some games, buying tiles from the stock is allowed. In this case, a player draws the number of tiles he is permitted to take according to the rules of that game, adding them to the tiles he is holding in his hand. Once the player has drawn a tile he is able to play, he plays that domino.

There are many domino games that have the rule that all tiles in the stock may be bought, and there are others that have the rule that some tiles must be left in the stock and cannot be bought. In the case of the latter, the number of pips on the tiles left in the stock at the end of the game are added to the winner's score.

Line of Play

There are many domino games that depend upon matching suits. In these games, the first player sets his domino, then the player to his left adds his tile to one of the free ends, and so on, going clockwise around the table with each player adding a tile. Players add tiles that have the matching number of pips with an open end of an already played tile.

As each player matches and plays a tile, a line is formed. This configuration of dominoes is called the layout, string, or line of play. In order to prevent tiles from falling off the table when the line of play extends too far, dominoes may be played in any direction. Regardless of the pattern of the line of play, the open end of the last domino played remains the same.

Dominoes are joined to the line of play in two 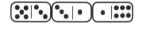 ways: (1) with the line of play, lengthwise (dominoes played end to end) or (2) across the line of play, crosswise (dominoes played across the matching number). In most domino games, doubles and *only* doubles are played crosswise; singles are played lengthwise. The next tile added after each double played, if the double is not a spinner, must be lengthwise.

Spinners: A spinner is a double that can be played on all four sides. Depending on the rules of the game being played, the double played as the lead is the only spinner of the game; *or* every double played throughout the game is a spinner. If

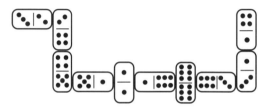

the double played is not a spinner, it may be played on only two sides.

Scoring: In some domino games, part of the score is obtained from the total number of pips at the ends of the line of play as the game progresses. If only one domino has been played, both ends of that domino are ends of the line of play. Thus, if a 5-5 tile is played, the count would be 10.

If two dominoes have been played, the count depends on whether both tiles are with the line of play or one tile is with and the other tile is across the line of play. For example, if the 3-5 and 5-1 tiles are played, the count is 4 (3+1). The matching halves of each of the two dominoes would be joined, end to end, with the open ends being 3 and 1). If the 3-5 and 5-5 tiles are played, the count is 13 (3+5+5). The double tile, 5-5, would be played across the line of play, and both halves of the double would be considered ends of the line of play.

Given the last example, if a tile is now played on the 5-5, assuming it is not a spinner, the 5-5 is no longer an end for the purpose of counting. See the example below. The line of play is 3-5, 5-5, 5-1, and the count is 4 (3+1). If the 5-5 is not a spinner in this case, the 5-5 is not an end.

In some domino games, a score is made only when the count of the ends of the line of play is a multiple of 5 or a multiple of 3, for example.

Another scoring method used in many domino games is to take the losing players' total number of pips by counting the pips on the tiles left in their hands at the end of a hand or the game and then adding that number to the winner's score.

Here is a rule variation that players may agree to employ: When counting the pips on the tiles left in the losers' hands at the end of a hand or the game, count only one end of a double (e.g., 4-4 counts as only 4 points).

End of the Game

Some domino games end once a certain number of hands have been played or a player or team makes the necessary points to win. For many other domino games, the object of the game is to be the first player (or team) to dispose of all the dominoes in hand. These domino games end when a player has played all the dominoes in his or her hand and summarily announces, "Domino."

Sometimes none of the players are able to make another play. This is called a *blocked game*, and, in case the game is blocked and no one is able to make another play, the game would end.

If Accidents Occur

During a game, there will be times when errors or misplays will occur. Here are general rules for handling some common accidents.

Dominoes exposed in error: If your domino is accidentally exposed to another player, it must then be exposed to all of the players.

Too many tiles drawn: If a player draws more tiles for his hand than he is entitled to, it is called an *overdraw*. Once an overdraw has been discovered, the player to the right of the overdrawn hand takes the extra dominoes from the overdrawn hand, without looking at them, and returns them to the stock. The deck should then be reshuffled before anyone else draws his hand. (Here is a rule variation that players may agree to employ: Expose the overdrawn tiles to all players before returning them to the stock and then reshuffle the deck.)

Not enough tiles drawn: If a player draws fewer tiles than he or she is entitled to for a hand, it is called an *underdraw*. Once an underdraw has been discovered, the player draws the necessary tiles from the stock to complete the hand.

Domino played in error: When a player plays the wrong domino, it is called a *misplay*. If a player misplays (for example, joins a 2 to a 3) and it is discovered before the next play is made, the misplayer must restore the incorrect tile to his hand and play a correct one. If a player misplays and no one notices until after the next play has been made, the wrong tile is considered played and cannot be replaced with the correct tile. If a score is realized on the undiscovered misplay, the player is allowed to keep it.

If a play is not a misplay, once a tile is played and a player takes his hand off the tile, it may not be taken up again by the player.

Play out of turn: When a player plays out of turn, it is also called a misplay. If a player plays out of turn and it is discovered before the next player makes his play, he must recall his tile. If a player plays out of turn and it is not discovered before the next play, the misplay must stand. If a score is realized on the misplay, the player is allowed to keep it.

Types of Domino Games

Nearly all of the most popular domino games fit into one of four categories: bidding games, blocking games, scoring games, and round games.

Bidding games: Bidding games are cardlike games, played by two to four players. In these games, players bid their hands, the highest bidder names the suit, and the score is determined by the bid

Blocking games: Blocking games are played by matching dominoes in a line. Scoring is done only at the end of each hand. The player or team that plays all the dominoes in their hand first, or "dominoes," scores the total count of the tiles still held by his opponent(s). In the event of a blocked game, the player or team who has the lowest count scores the total count of the tiles still held by his opponent(s).

Scoring games: A scoring game, like a blocking game, is also played by matching dominoes. One difference is that scoring is done throughout the game after each scoring play is made, as well as at the end of each hand. The game is played until a player or team makes the necessary points to win. A game consists of a series of hands. A hand consists of a series of plays with the dominoes drawn from the deck.

Round Games: Round games are: (1) "Party games" for a large group of people. (2) Games in which each player plays for himself.

Intermediate Skills

If you are a novice player you may need to read no further. I am sure that you can enjoy countless hours of fun playing this game with the basic skills covered already. Dominoes then becomes mostly a game of "a little luck and a lotta fun."

Somehow I know this will not satisfy you. You bought this book because you want to become a better-than-average player, or better yet, a champion domino player. If this is so, then read on.

After a few games are played (or observed), the smart player realizes that he can improve his odds of winning by a few simple strategies. Paraphrasing Isaac Asimov's Laws of Robotics, I present the "Three

Laws of Dominotics." These laws help you win the game by guiding you in two ways: making your opponents pass, and making sure you don't pass.

First Law: A domino player must develop his own strong suits and help his partner develop his.

Second Law: A domino player must prevent the development of the opponents' strong suits, as long as this does not conflict with the first law.

Third Law: A domino player should play his tiles so as not to yield a suit, as long as this does not interfere with the first and second laws.

The First Law states you must develop your strong suit, this being the one you have the most of. For example, if your hand looks like this:

the 4s are your strong suit.

You develop the strong suit by playing it and by not covering it unless forced to do so. If you have many tiles of one particular suit, then your opponents must have few of them and may be forced to pass (if they have none).

The Second Law states you must prevent the development of your opponents' strong suits. This is achieved by covering their suits with your tiles, and by *not* playing those numbers for them. If possible, you should also keep the opponents from playing their suits, usually by attacking them with your own.

This interference is always carried out unless it conflicts with the development of your own strengths (First Law).

The Third Law states you should keep from yielding a suit in your hand. To "yield a suit" means that after playing a tile you now have no other of that particular suit. For example, if you hold only the [domino] [domino] [domino] and need to play on a 4, then play the [domino]; you still keep in your hand another 4 and another 3. If you play the [domino], then you yield the 1s and next time that you're threatened by a 1 you'll have to pass.

Playing to prevent yielding a suit should be subordinated to the first two laws. In other words, it is not as important as developing your strong suit or preventing the opponents from developing theirs.

Mental Exercises

Here are two fundamental abilities the domino player needs in order to excel. First and foremost is excellent memory, which is used to gather information about the game as it is being played. The second is the ability to take that information and, using deduction, figure out what is the best play to make from the tiles in one's hand.

An experienced player can usually tell, at any point in the game, who played a particular tile and in what order it was played. To help you do the same, I've written down the following mental exercises to develop your ability to recall.

These exercises are arranged in order of increasing difficulty. It will take some time to get good at them, but if you practice hard enough, the results will be self-evident when you rack up more wins.

1. When it's your turn to play, reconstruct the skeleton on the table, both the order as well as which player laid each tile.
2. Have another player pick any tile on the board at random, then try to remember who played it.
3. At the end of a game, pick up your original seven tiles from the skeleton.
4. Alternatively, pick up your partner's seven tiles.
5. Finally, pick up both of your opponents' original seven tiles.

Another important skill is to be able to count the number of points on the board at any time in the game. Remember that the total number of points in the 28 tiles equals 168, so you can also know how many points are *unplayed* by subtracting:

$$168 - \text{played points} = \text{unplayed points}$$

This is helpful for two reasons. If a jam is contemplated, then knowing how many points are in the players' hands can be of critical importance. You can also astound your fellow players with a variation of this skill. I remember playing with an

80-year-old man who could keep a running total of the played tiles so that after the game was over he could nonchalantly announce the points won before I could even count the tiles. Now that's impressive at any age!

Analyzing Your Hand

The seven tiles you pick at the beginning of a game are your weapons in the upcoming battle. You should therefore study them carefully prior to playing the first one. If you analyze their combined strengths and weaknesses you can determine the initial strategy to follow.

The tiles can be reorganized after you get them, arranged in such a way that the suits are next to each other. This can help you "see" what you have in your hand.

Consider the following tiles in the hand of the leadoff player in our first sample game (Chapter 3):

The strength of this hand is not readily apparent. If you reorganize them in this fashion,

then it's easier to see that you have five 2s. There are only two others left in this suit, so there is a good chance you can make the other players pass by playing the 2s. You also observe you have no 1s. These can make you pass and must be avoided. Your initial strategy should therefore be to develop your 2s, while trying to prevent the development of the 1s.

Let's consider another hand:

After you reorganize them,

it's easier to see that this is a game with no particular strengths, but many weaknesses. There are no more than two of each suit represented, there are no 1s or blanks, and there are four doubles. As a general rule, the more doubles a hand has, the tougher it will be to win by dominating the game. This particular hand is also "heavy," or loaded with points.

Not every game can be won, and this hand really looks like a loser. The strategy here should consist of minimizing the possible damage, discarding as many of the points as possible. Since you can't mount an offensive campaign, you should support your partner's hand even at the expense of your own.

Here's another sample hand (after reorganizing):

This hand is lacking in 6s, but is strongest in 1s and blanks. You should be thinking not only of developing the 1s and blanks, but also of the possibility of jamming the game. Having few total points means you are at an advantage if a jam arises.

A last example:

This hand has no particular strengths, having no more than two of any suit, but at least there are no suits missing. Although you can't mount an effective attack on your own, you can support your partner in his offensive and effectively thwart the development of your opponents' suits.

I should warn you that this technique of reorganizing the tiles in order to analyze your hand should be abandoned as more experience is gained. Some competitions forbid the shifting around of the tiles after picking them up. Worse yet, "shark" players can make very astute deductions about your tiles according to how you organize them and from where you play them. Notice, for example, how doubles often end up at the right or left end.

The Leadoff

The leadoff is a distinct advantage for the team that has it, since it allows them to develop their tiles first. For the lead player it can serve one of two purposes:

1. To start the attack with your strongest suit. This number will be the one your partner will try to support, while your opponents attempt to thwart its development. It is assumed (but not known for sure) that you have at least one other tile of this suit.

2. To discard from your hand a tile that is dangerous, either because it interferes with the development of your strong suit, or because it's a double you fear may end up getting hung. As a general rule, players usually lead with the heaviest double in their hand in order to discard points and to ensure they don't get stuck with that tile.

Both purposes may be achieved by the playing of the same tile. For example, if your hand is as follows:

then leading with the begins to develop the 5s as your strong suit and also gets rid of a potentially difficult double.

Keep these goals in mind as you determine the best leadoff tile in the following hands.

Example 1: No Doubles

This hand has no double tiles. Its main defect is not having any 6s. Observing that there are three 4s and three 2s, you realize a lead with the [2|4] can develop the two strongest suits in your hand.

Leading with anything other than a double tile is called an "open lead." The other players will figure that the lead player either has no doubles to get rid of or has decided to keep the doubles for some particular reason. Subsequent plays will make clear which is correct.

Lead with the [2|4].

Example 2: One Double

If you have two, three, or four tiles of a suit,

including the double, then the logical leadoff is with the double itself. The only way a double in your hand can't be hung is if you have four or more additional tiles of the same suit. Even three others are not enough to be assured of its safety. You could play all three of them and they might all be covered by your next play. In this case, leading with the 🁡 not only assures it will not be hung, but also begins to develop your strongest suit.

The best lead is the 🁡.

Example 3: One Double

To lead with a double when you have no other tiles of that suit (for example, the ⬜ in the above hand) is called "leading a bluff." Although you are discarding a double, such a lead can sometimes be a poor move for several reasons. First, it sends the wrong message to your partner, and he might try to develop the blanks thinking it is your strong suit. Second, you lose the only blank you have (yielding the suit). Third, you may be leading with what may actually be the opponents' strong suit; in this case not only do you facilitate their play, but you lose what would have been an excellent tile to have in your hand. Finally, leading with the [1] doesn't allow you to lighten up your point load, which could be important if a jam develops.

An open lead with one of the three 4s seems advisable. All things being equal, you should lead with the ⚅⚃, since there is another 6 in the hand and since it's the heaviest tile in the hand. Later in the game, if your partner sees you play the [1], he should surmise that you have no other blanks (or you would have led with it) and must therefore protect you against them.

You should lead with the ⚅⚃.

Example 4: One Double

Here your strong suit is the 5s, but the ⚅⚅ is a

59

thorn in your side. A lead with it might not seem to be the most straightforward play. Leading with this double, however, would not be a bluff lead (since you have another 6), and it would eliminate the one bad tile in the hand. If you are forced to later cover the 6, you can do so with the [6|5] and attack with your 5s.

Leading with the [6|6] is a strong play.

Example 5: One Double

A dream of a hand! Five of a kind, with no other doubles and no suits missing. There are two possible ways to lead it.

The first is to lead with the [1|1]. This way the other players must play a 1, maybe even both 1s that are missing, which would put you in great position with all the remaining 1s in your hand. There's even a good chance you will make the 2nd-lead pass immediately. It's a solid play and can't be faulted.

You could play otherwise, and lead with the ⊞[I •]. The [• I •] in your hand can't be hung, and you also develop your blanks. This will initially make the other players think you have no doubles, and hides the devastating power of the 1s to come. If you're later forced to cover your 1s, you have the double to use. Playing the [• I •] in the middle of the game will also tell your partner that you had *more* than four 1s to begin with, and none of the suit on the other side of the skeleton (or you would not have doubled then).

It's probably better to lead with the [I •].

Example 6: Two Doubles

You have in your hand a [dom] and a [dom]. It's not a memorable group of tiles. Since you have two other 4s, and only one other 6, a good option is to lead with the [dom]. Your hope is that, since you don't have the [dom], perhaps another player will play it and allow you to double with the ⬛. Since you usually lead with the heaviest double in your hand, however, this might mistakenly tell your partner you don't have anything heavier than the ⬛ in your hand. Should you lead then with the ⬛?

This is a hard choice to make and neither lead is wrong.

Example 7: Two Doubles

This is an easier choice. The 5s are clearly your stronger suit, and a lead with the ⬛ develops them. It's unfortunate that you have the ⬛ in your hand, but with a little luck you may still get to play it. You could lead with the ⬛ and hope someone covers it with the ⬛ (giving you a devastating advantage in 5s), but this is less likely.

The ⬛ is the best lead.

Example 8: Three or Four Doubles

This is a terrible hand, where you hope your partner has good tiles and will "pull the hand" (take over the offensive of the team—see "Pulling the Hand," page 109). The best lead might be a double, but not a bluff one. The ⚃ is by default the best choice, since it doesn't yield a suit.

Alternatively, there is a lead that has been popularized by William Almodovar. You lead with a non-double, *if* you still keep in your hand the doubles that match both ends. From the above example, this would be the ⚂ because you hold the ⚃ and the ⚁ in your hand.

This is tricky, since your partner must figure out your hand if there is to be a chance of winning. When you lead with an open tile, your partner examines his tiles. If he doesn't have either of the doubles, he can suspect an Almodovar's Opening; when the 2nd-lead doesn't double, your partner is almost assured you have those doubles. He can therefore play so you have opportunities to discard those doubles, or may decide his hand is best and pull the hand.

You should lead with the ⸬⁚⸬.

Example 9: Five or More Doubles

In my youth, it was often said that you could fold a hand (rescramble the tiles) only if you had eight doubles. This of course meant you played with whatever hand you were dealt. Now that I'm older, and of a more delicate disposition, I'm happy that the rules allow folding a hand and rescrambling if you have five (or more) doubles. It's healthier for my blood pressure.

Nevertheless, you may be feeling adventurous or invincible and want to play this hand. If so, here's a tip I once garnered long ago: Lead with an open tile, if possible, in which you *don't* have either of those two doubles. It's the opposite from the Almodovar's Opening. The confusion you'll cause and the expression on the other players' faces as you play double after double may be the highlight of the match. Lead with the ⸬:, sit back, and enjoy the ride!

Keeping Track of the Tiles

It is important to be able to keep track of the tiles as the skeleton is built. This applies both to the played and unplayed tiles, and both your team's as well as your opponents'.

Consider again the lead player's hand in the first sample game:

Not only is he aware of the five 2s he has, he should also realize the ⸬ and the ⸬ are the missing 2s. As the game is played, he keeps looking out for their appearance. He should also try to get them played as quickly as possible, so he'll have the last 2s left (First Law—develop your strong suit).

If you also keep track of the opponents' tiles, you may prevent their attacks (Second Law—obstruct the opponents' suits). Here's an example.

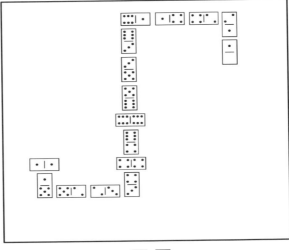

At this stage of the game you've figured out the player to your right (following you) is attacking with the 4s. You now must play a blank, and if your opponent plays a 4 and attacks, you will lose. Which one should you play?

Looking at the board you can see there are five 4s played and two missing, the ⟨4|4⟩ and the ⟨4|1⟩. If you double with the ⟨4|4⟩, the ⟨4|1⟩ can be played and you'll lose. Playing the ⟨4|1⟩ guarantees that no 4 can attack at that moment.

Blocking the opponents' plays can only be effectively carried out if you constantly keep track of those tiles not played.

Here's another example.

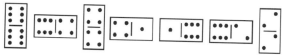

You are the runt and are holding

in your hand. The opponents led with the ⟨4|4⟩. Your partner played the first 1, and you'd like to help him develop this suit. How can you help him to play the 1s?

Keeping track of the tiles you don't have, you realize there are four 1s unaccounted for: these are the [5|1], the [6|1], the [4|1], and the [1|1]. If you play either the [1|5] or the [1|2], there is a chance your tile might be covered with a 4 (the [5|4] and the [1|4] are missing) and your partner would be faced with a 6 on one side and with a 4 on the other. He wouldn't be able to play a 1 (the [3|1] and the [2|1] are already played).

If you cover the 6 with the [3|6] then both ends of the skeleton give him the opportunity to play a 1, either the [6|1] or the [4|1]. The next player can't cover both ends in one play.

Now for a final example (See opposite.):

Let's say that your partner holds the door to the blanks (the last one), and you think your team can win a jam. Looking at the skeleton you should be able to tell the door is the [0|1]. In that case, you can play the [2|1] instead of the [2|6], hoping the next player may not have a 1 (or might double on it) and your partner can then jam the game with the [0|1].

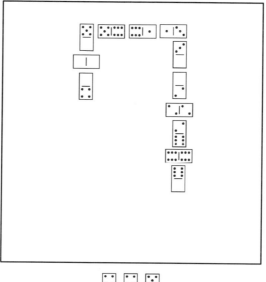

However, if the player after you holds the door and you think you'd lose the jam, play the ![domino] to prevent it.

Cover, Repeat, and Square

The phrase "cover, repeat, and square" is often heard when beginners are first taught the strategy of the game. It is a very simplistic theory and yet it underlies most of the plays. If we were to compare dominoes with playing basketball, for example, then the equivalent strategy would be to say that to play it you need to "block, dribble, and shoot." Obviously basketball is more than those strategies, and yet how can you win unless you're able to do them well?

Cover: This means to play a domino tile on one side of the skeleton to cover that particular number. What is this number you are supposed to cover? The number to cover is the strong suit of your opponents.

Here's an example:

In this game you started as the runt, or last

player. The lead player led with the ⚂⚃ and the 3rd-lead has just played the ⚀⚁. Since the opponents appear to be playing the 3s, and there's a 3 on one side of the skeleton, then it's logical you should "cover" this number with a tile of your own. If you don't do so, the lead player might be able to play a 3 and make your partner pass, or they might end up with a crucial door.

If your partner has no 3s, he'll be forced to play on the other side of the skeleton. In doing so, he may not be able to develop his hand, or perhaps he'll be forced to cover his own strong suit. He might have to play a tile that allows the next opponent to attack—and then it might be your turn to pass.

What if the only 3 you have is the ⚂⚃ and it's also the only 4? You should not worry about yielding two suits (Third Law). Preventing the development of the opponents' suit (Second Law) is a higher priority.

What if you see the opponents developing a suit and you realize you might be able to play that same suit yourself? In the above example, what if you had in your hand both the ⬛ as well as the ⬛? You might decide not to cover but to leave the 3 open, hoping to keep one or both of the doors.

This style of play is called "building a house." It means you abandon your partner to the tender mercies of the opponents, trying to get them to play for you without realizing it. The danger is that you can't expect much help from your partner, since he might now be unable to develop his game and still be trying to thwart the 3s from being played. We will discuss this style of playing in Chapter 14. For now, understand that the straightforward player would expect you to cover that 3 to follow the Second Law.

Covering prevents the development of the opponents' dangerous suits, and is therefore a *defensive* move (Second Law).

Repeat: This means to play a domino tile on one side of the skeleton to present a number for the second (or third) time. Here you're trying to play to your own or your partner's strong suit. (The numbers above the dominoes indicate the order in which they were played.)

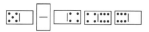

In this sample game, the lead player started with the ▢. At the first opportunity he had, he "repeated," playing the ▢. This signals to everybody that his strong suit is the blanks.

Not unexpectedly, the 2nd-lead doesn't have any more blanks and is forced to play on the 5. He has two of them, the ▢ and the ▢. He thinks a little before playing (to let his partner know he has at least one other 5), then plays the ▢. He is repeating his 4s, since his first play was the ▢.

The ▢ would be a weak play, since it would allow the next player to repeat the blanks if he has the ▢. On the other hand, repeating the 4s with the ▢ ensures that the 3rd-lead won't be able to do so, since the ▢ has already been played. Since it's the second time the 3rd-lead sees the 4, it might be too strong for him; he might not have any more 4s and be forced to cover his partner's blank.

What if the ⚃ is the last 4 that the 2nd-lead has? Should he repeat the suit even if it's not his strongest one? This is a tough situation, and you can play it one of two ways.

You can think for a long while before playing this tile. When your partner sees you repeating (and knows that this is usually a good move) he'll understand that if you had to think about it, there was something about the play you didn't like. You either wanted to play a double, but decided that repeating was a better move, or else you have no more 4s. If your partner understands your hesitation, he can study his own tiles and decide if he has the majority of the 4s or not. It is then his decision whether to proceed with their development or not.

Otherwise, after thinking about it for a while, play some other 5. Your partner will understand that either: a) you don't have the ⚃, or else b) you have it but the 4s might not be your strongest suit. Either way, the long "thought" tells him you had problems deciding the best play to make, and alerts him to potential trouble in your hand.

Repeating is the best way to develop a strong suit, and is an *offensive* move (First Law).

Square: This is the most powerful weapon you have to make an opponent pass. "Squaring" means you play a tile so both sides of the skeleton have the same suit. The tile you use to do so is known as the squaring tile, or ST. For example:

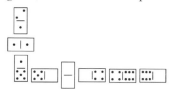

You're the leadoff player and you led with the ☐ ☐ . If you play the ☐ on the 2, now both sides of the skeleton have a blank. You have "squared to blank."

If you have another blank in your hand (like the ☐ , for example), then there is only one other unaccounted for. Chances are that you will make the next player pass, and you'll be sitting pretty with the door to the blanks.

Squaring is the most effective way of developing a suit. This is why the opponents should always try to prevent you from doing it. It is also the most effective way of thwarting your opponents. Consider if the above game had developed in the following way:

You led with the blanks, and repeated with the ⬛. The 2nd-lead now repeats his 4 with the ⬛, and your partner has to cover your blank with the ⬛. The runt now squares to 4 with the ⬛.

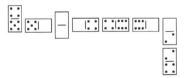

This square was extremely powerful. It prevents

you from playing a blank and attacking. Your partner doesn't have any more 4s, or he wouldn't have covered your blank with the [⡇•]. If you don't have any 4s, you now pass and lose the lead player position. Worse yet, the opponents will be able to play the [⠿⠿] (most likely in the 2nd-lead's hand), and retain two doors!

Sometimes you're forced to square not to your strong suit but to the opponent's. Here's an example:

[⠿|⠿] [•|⠿⠇] [⠿⠿|⠿⠇]

You're the runt. You have the [⠿⠇•] in your hand and must play it, since you have no more 1s or 3s. Do you square with the lead player (who led the [•|•]) to 1s, or with the 3rd-lead to 3s?

It may be satisfying to square to 1 and watch the lead player have to cover his own suit. Unless you suspect he led a bluff, that's about all the satisfaction you're going to get out of this play.

If you square to 3, you know your partner

won't have to face another 1 this round. It's possible you might even make the lead player pass, making your partner the new lead player. The [domino] will come out, though, and it's usually in the hand of the opponent who played the 3 first.

Either way, you see the square in this situation is a weak play. I usually square with the 3rd-lead (to 3 in this example), and hope to make the lead player pass.

Here's another situation. You're the lead player now, and must square with one opponent or another. (Again, the numbers above the dominoes indicate the order in which they were played.)

You hold the [domino] and it's your only tile in either suit. Should you square to the 2nd-lead's 5s, or to the runt's blanks?

One answer is that, if you're the lead player, the one who can hurt you (make you pass) is the runt and you should therefore square *against* him by playing on the blank end.

You hope that by the time the play comes back to you, the 5s may be covered up again. Of course, the ![domino] will come out and your partner probably doesn't have it. Indeed, a common occurrence is that the 2nd-lead doubles with the ![domino], and your partner passes to 5s. Now the last player must cover the 5 and you'll have a different suit to play on.

Another way is to square to the runt by playing on the 5. It's likely your partner has a blank, since he hasn't played any yet. The ![domino] is probably in the runt's hand; the 2nd-lead will either pass or play a fresh tile to your partner. If the 2nd-lead does play a blank, for example the ![domino], your partner should now cover the blank on the other side of the skeleton immediately. This opens the game for you to continue developing your suit.

Which opponent you square with depends on the strength of your hand. If you think you can win it, you'll square with the player following you, even if your partner gets in trouble. If your hand is not a strong one, you'll square with the player preceding you in order to open the game for your partner. And if you do the latter, and your partner knows your strategy of the game, he'll understand you're telling him, "My game isn't great. I'd rather you lead, if you can."

Squaring can therefore be seen as both an *offensive* as well as a *defensive* strategy.

Advanced Skills

Communicating with Your Partner

Very infrequently your hand can be so strong, so overpowering that you can win on the strength of your tiles alone. Most games, however, are won when your tiles and those of your partner can complement each other. In this fashion a team can make the opponents pass more often, while your team may develop two or even three suits.

By now you've gathered that a lot of decision-making involved in playing dominoes requires you to have at least an idea of the tiles that the other players have in their hands. This is not an easy matter. The opponents won't tell you, and sometimes will make plays to confuse you. Your partner is the only one with a vested interest in conveying to you the contents of his hand. How can you tell each other the tiles in your hands?

The one allowed way to convey information between partners is by the act of thinking—specifically, how long it takes you to play a tile is supposed to tell something about your hand. Of course, in order to understand each other, you and your partner must use the same "thinking conventions." Let's explore how you can use this tool.

You first begin to use it with your lead. If you only have one double, and it's going to be your lead tile, then play it quickly. This tells your partner, "My game is fairly good. I may have no other double."

A medium-length "thought" before leading a double says: "I have more than one double and my game is fair but may not be very strong."

A prolonged thought followed by a double tells

the partner you either have a lot of doubles (3 or 4), and have a poor hand, or you might have led a bluff (not having any others of the suit whose double you just played) for reasons to be determined as the game progresses.

A prolonged thought followed by leading with an open tile (one with a different suit in each end) says you either have a poor game with many doubles—and decided to use Almodovar's Opening—or you may truly have no doubles in your hand and yet were unsure which was the best lead. Perhaps you did have one double in your hand with no others of that suit, toyed with the idea of leading a bluff, but decided not to.

All this information can be (legally) expressed simply by varying the time used to think before playing the leadoff tile. Of course, the opponents will also pick up this information, and will try to use it against you. I still believe it is more important to let your partner know your hand, since he's the only one who has an interest in helping you.

Thinking time is used throughout the game, not just to lead off. For example, if the lead player leads with a ⬛ and you, as the 2nd-lead, have only one 5, then play it quickly. This tells your partner he needs to cover the 5 as soon as he can. Your tile was a forced play, so the suit you show may not be your strong one.

If you think on the ⬛, then it means you have two 5s—maybe even three if you think for at least ten seconds. Since you took the time to decide which 5 to play, the tile you played is probably your strongest suit and your partner should help in its development. He also shouldn't feel forced to cover the ⬛ that the lead player led with, since you have at least one other to defend yourself with.

Let's follow a game for two rounds, to see this concept in action. You're supposed to lead and, after thinking for about five to ten seconds, you play the ⬛. This tells your partner you have at least one other double. You probably didn't lead a bluff, or you would have thought for a little longer before leading.

The 2nd-lead, after a brief pause, plays the [6|6]. If he's playing with the "thinking time" conventions, then you assume he probably has another 6. Remember, though, you can only truly trust your partner; the opponent could be bluffing. Your partner now plays the [5|5] rapidly; this must be his only 5. The last player also plays the [6|1] rapidly.

You quickly play the [1|1]; your partner now knows what your other double was. The next player plays the [0|1]. The board now looks like this:

[1|0] [1|6] [6|6] [6|5] [5|1] [0|1]

Now your partner thinks, and thinks some more. Then he plays the [0|6]. What does this mean?

He knew the [0|6] was a good move, since it would have repeated your leadoff suit, developing the 6s. And yet he was reluctant to play it. This must mean he had other blanks, and he must have really hated covering the [0|1]. Perhaps he even

85

has the [|]. If so, he made a decision: he's sacri-
ficing a strong suit, even putting his [|] at risk
of getting hung, to support your hand. You now
start considering how to get him to play his blanks,
especially if you happen to have some in your hand.
This is how partners can help each other and, in so
doing, defeat their opponents.

What if you need to think because you have
choices on both ends of the skeleton? For example,
you hold the [⚃⚁] [⚁⚀] [⚁⚀] in your hand and the
skeleton looks like this:

You need to consider whether to play a 4 or a 2. If
you decide to play a 4, like the [⚁⚁], then a
moderate pause to think before playing it conveys
the message that you have other 4s. If you decide
to play the [⚁⚀], but realize the time you took to
think this over will make your partner believe you
have other 2s, then simply play the [⚁⚀] *quickly*.
That is, take the tile in a quick movement and place

it on the table with a definite, short action. The meaning of the quick action will be plainly understood: it's your only 2.

Sometimes it's okay to think even when you have no other choice but one play. It should be done to fool the opponents, when possible. Here's an example:

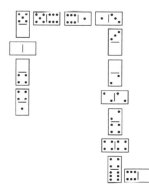

You suspect the player after you has the door to the blanks, the ▢•| . The only play you have is the ▢•|• , which will allow him to jam the game. You also estimate that the opponents will win this jam.

You can bluff by thinking, then playing the [•|•]
—which may cause the opponent to fear you could
be setting him up—and therefore decide *not* to jam!
Here's another example, where you can fool the
opponents without confusing your partner.

Let's say both opponents have passed on the 1, so
they know you and your partner have the three 1s
left. It's your turn and you are forced to cover your
strong suit with your only 1, the [•|•]. If you play
it quickly then the opponents will know your
partner has the last two 1s left, and can play to
prevent him from playing them. By thinking for a
while on your play, you can fool them into believing
you have at least another 1, and your partner is
amused by what he knows is only a trick.

This last setup can have another effect. If your
partner plays one of the 1s he has left, the opponents
will believe you must have the door and may unwit-
tingly make it possible for him to jam the game!

You need to be careful of not only what tile you play, but also the speed with which you play it. You might have only one play possible, but if you stop to think about what has just been played, or what possible effect your play will have, then your partner believes you have choices to make. Still, you need to keep up with the development of the game. This is crucial.

How then can you achieve both goals; that is, use "thinking" to convey information while carefully analyzing the plays made? You do this by anticipating the tiles that may be played, much as the chess player figures out the next several moves he can make.

Playing the Doubles

The doubles often play a crucial part in a game. By nature, they are defensive tiles. They can't be used by themselves to attack an opponent or cover their suit, but they can keep the present suit unchanged. They can also get hung, becoming unplayable.

Playing the doubles correctly sometimes leaves the realm of pure logic and begins to enter that of instinct. Here is where dominoes truly becomes a game of finesse and "gut feeling." Still, certain general principles about their play can be discussed.

When to Play the Double

Doubles are usually bad tiles to have in your hand. There are players who believe the team that has picked up four or more doubles should theoretically lose. Five or more doubles in one player's hand even allows him to ask for a new hand.

This means that, as a general rule, you should discard the doubles as soon as the opportunity arises. Consider the following example: you're the 3rd-lead. Your teammate led with the [tile]. The 2nd-lead plays the [tile]. If you have the [tile], it should be played at this time. If you have this tile and don't play it, your partner will assume it's in one of the opponents' hands and will try to hang it.

Can you estimate the probability that a double in your hand will get hung? You can get a feel for it by looking at the rest of the tiles. Consider the following examples:

Here the is the only 6 you have. There are six others out there in the other players' hands. It is unlikely the will get hung, and it may even keep you from passing if you're attacked with the 6s.

Having another 6 in the hand increases the chances of getting the hung, especially since the is your only 4, and you may be forced to play it on a 4 in the skeleton.

Two or three others with the double represent the highest danger. Three others is somewhat less than two, because if your partner can play just one 6, then you'll be assured of doubling. If the others are all in the opponents' hands, however, then any 6 you play can be covered and you might never get the chance to play the ⬛⬛.

With four others, there is now no way your opponents can hang the double. Only you yourself can do it.

When Not to Play the Double

We've established that doubles are usually to be discarded at the first opportunity. Are there situations when you'd like to play them, but probably shouldn't? Yes, if a) there is a better play to make, or b) doubling would allow something bad to happen.

Here's an example. You, as the fourth player, are given the chance to double on the 4. The lead player led with the ⬛⬛ and your partner played the ⬛⬛.

You have in your hand both the ⚃⚃ and the ⚃⚀. Your first instinct would be to double, and yet you realize the 4 has been played for the first time and will probably not seriously threaten the lead player. Repeating your partner's 1 would represent an attack, so the ⚃⚀ is a better play.

Consider also that the ⚃⚁ is not played yet. Since the lead player started with the ⚁⚁, you assume the 2s are his strong suit. If you double, he could the play the ⚃⚁, squaring to 2 and attacking your partner.

Here's another example later in the same game, where doubling at the wrong time could lead to disaster. You have the choice of playing the ⚃⚃ or playing the ⚃⚁.

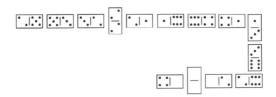

You're once again given the opportunity to double on the 4. This time the ⚂⚃ is not only missing—it's the jamming tile. You suspect your team would lose the jam so the ⚃⚂ is the best play possible.

The question may then be asked, is the only good double a dead double? Not necessarily—if it's the double of your team's strong suit. Having five of a suit, including the double, means you don't have to cover your own suit when attacked, since the double allows you to repeat it. It is thrilling when your partner squares to a strong suit, the opponent passes, then you double, repeating the attack and making the next opponent pass.

If you know a double won't be hung, doubling becomes optional. For example, let's say you're the fourth player and this is the skeleton:

Your tiles are:

Doubling up on the 3 might seem like a good idea, but the [3|2] is actually a powerful weapon in your hand. Since your partner has played two 3s in a row ([3|blank] and [3|3]), it is probably his strong suit. The better play is to cover the 2 on the right with the [2|3], squaring with your partner to the 3s. This play may force the leadoff player to pass, making your partner the new lead player. You'll hopefully get to play the [3|2] in the next round.

When to Pursue the Double

If getting your doubles hung is a potential disaster, then hanging your opponents' seems like a wise strategy. There are players who are experts at this aspect of the game, and will doggedly pursue doubles to the death. Some will carry this persecution of the double to an extreme, hanging any and all doubles they don't have. This may prevent them from developing their game and may even get their partners in trouble

How can you tell if you should hang a double or not? After all, if you're hanging a double, by definition you are throwing away the door to that suit that you might otherwise keep to yourself. As a general rule, if you're fairly certain your partner doesn't have that particular double, it's best to hang it.

Try to keep track of the doubles as the game is played. Here are two examples.

You are the 3rd-lead and your partner leads off with the ⬚⬚. If you had the ⬚⬚ in your hand you would play it, so your ⬚⬚ tells your partner (if he doesn't have it) it's in one of the opponents' hands. This is one double that your team shouldn't hesitate to hang.

⬚⬚ ⬚⬚ ⬚⬚ ⬚⬚ ⬚⬚

The runt plays the ⬚⬚, and your partner starts the second round with the ⬚⬚. Since he didn't double with the ⚃ then it means he doesn't have it and you can hang it with impunity, right? Not necessarily—he may have the double, but decided it was more important to repeat the attack with the 6s than to double, and he hopes to be able to discard it later. Further plays will show which of the two possibilities was correct.

When to Hang Your Own Double

As strange as it sounds, you are sometimes required to hang your own double—the ultimate sacrifice! You should do this only if it's needed for your partner to win.

Let's say your partner has one tile left, and you know it's the ⚃. On the board there is a 5 at one end of the skeleton; on the other end is a 1, and you hold the last two 1s (the ▢•|•▢ and the ▢•|•.▢). By hanging your own 1 and playing the ▢•|•.▢, you assure your partner's victory, since the skeleton now has a 5 at one end and a 3 at the other—and your partner can't be stopped with the ⚃ in his hand.

Another example is when your partner is the

lead player and he has the door to one end of the skeleton. You have the double and the door to the other side. If you double, you know your partner must discard his door, potentially costing him the game. You may then think that hanging your double might allow him to play on the other end of the skeleton, keeping his door for another round. This is not a sure thing, however. The player after you may still attack with his strong suit, and force your partner to discard the door anyway—making your sacrifice worthless.

You don't usually win by weakening yourself for the sake of your partner, but rather by you and your partner helping each other develop your strengths. You should therefore hang your own double only if you're somehow assured of a catastrophe if you don't. This is extremely difficult to predict beforehand, so you won't find yourself making the ultimate sacrifice often.

How Your Position Affects Your Game Plan

Should your game strategy be different if you're the lead player, 2nd-lead, 3rd-lead, or runt? On a very basic level you can think of the lead player and 2nd-lead as being the attacking players of each team, those who will first develop their strong suits. The 3rd-lead and runt are supportive players, who may need to sacrifice their own interests for the sake of their partners.

Although superficially correct, this generalization will not give you the consistent results that are needed in order to win. If this were true, the team would always win (or lose) according to the strength of the first two players, and this is definitely not the case. Let's therefore consider each position one at a time in more detail.

The Attacking Players
Lead Player
The lead player is the only one who has the luxury

of choosing from all seven of his tiles and playing the one that helps him most. This advantage can't be taken lightly and choosing the correct tile to lead off must be done carefully.

If the tile he leads with is his strong suit (instead of playing to get rid of a bad double), then he must try to develop that suit. He must repeat it in order to keep the 2nd-lead off balance, hopefully until he passes. At that point his team becomes both lead player and 2nd-lead and his chances of winning increase significantly.

When feasible, he should try not to yield a suit (Third Law of Dominotics). He will therefore have a wider choice of plays and a better chance of preventing a pass.

Since few games can be won on the strength of one player only, he needs to look for opportunities to help develop his partner's tiles. If his hand is strong and he must choose between his partner's suit or his own, however, he'll prefer to develop his own game.

If his hand is weak, then he might discard the

heaviest double as a leadoff, and somehow let his partner know he is in trouble. In this situation, it is he who should support his partner (the initial 3rd-lead) in the development of his hand.

2nd-Lead

The 2nd-lead has to play off of the leading tile; his choices are more limited. He should still try to develop his strong suit as soon as possible, but he may not be able to do so until the following round, since he may be playing his first tile as a forced play.

If possible, the first tile he plays should be either his strong suit or a suit in which he holds a double (sometimes it's both at the same time). For example, if he holds the in his hand, and the lead was the , then a good play would be the .

He also should try not to yield a suit. He may need to do so, however, if it helps in the development of his team's strong suit.

Like the lead player, he should attempt to help

his partner (the runt) by repeating his strong suit. Squaring to his partner's suit, especially if it's against his own, is the best way to say he'd like for the runt to take over the offensive. For example:

The leadoff was the [domino]. You, as the 2nd-lead, played the [domino], and your partner, the runt, played the [domino]. At this stage of the game (third round) you hold the squaring tile, the [domino]. You know your game is weak and you'd like for the runt to take over the attack. You can do so by squaring to 2 (his first tile played) instead of to the 1s you first played. He'll understand immediately that you want him to take over.

The Defensive Players
3rd-Lead
The 3rd-lead's main responsibility is to assist his lead-player partner. His first play is defensive, but

he needs to begin showing his game and, if possible, his doubles.

The leadoff was the , and the 2nd-lead played the . If the 3rd-lead has the , he needs to play it now; otherwise his partner will assume he doesn't have it and may try to hang it. If he doesn't have it, he should play his strong suit that has a double; for example the if he has the (and maybe other 4s).

In the next few plays he needs to continually scan for weakness in his partner, to know whether he should take over the offensive (a strategy called "pulling the hand"). If so, he starts to play as if he were the lead player, and the lead-player guidelines apply to him.

If no signs of weakness are apparent, then he's expected to fully support the lead player. One way he does this is by repeating his partner's strong suit.

For example:

The 3rd-lead knows his partner, the lead player, played first the [5|4] and later the [6|5]. The 4 could be the lead player's strong suit, since he led with it. He could have been, however, discarding a bad tile, so maybe the 5s are his suit (being the second tile he played). How should the 3rd-lead play now?

If he has the [4|4] then he should play it, since he's repeating the lead to 4s. If he doesn't have it but has the [4|5], he can repeat the second suit his partner played (the 5). If he has neither, but has the [4|6] or the [5|6], then he should play one of them because he's now repeating his own first tile (the 6). If he has none of these, then he should play a double. If he plays *anything else* then the players should assume he has none of the above tiles. (*Note:* this is how you begin to guess the tiles in the hands of the other players—if they're playing logically! More about this in "How to Locate the Unplayed Tiles," page 117)

The runt is in the best position to make the lead player pass or discard a door. The 3rd-lead therefore has to prevent the runt from playing his strong suit. To do this, always keep in mind the tiles that are not in your hand (see page 65).

Finally, if he can't attack or prevent the opponents from attacking, then he should look for ways to help the lead player play his own strong suit. For example:

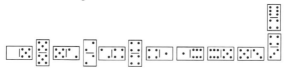

In the continuation of the above game, let's say that the 3rd-lead has figured out that his partner did have a strong game to 4s, and he suspects that the lead player has in his hand the last two 4s. Looking at the skeleton he can figure out that they are the [1:3] and the [4:3]. If he has the [6:1] in his hand and squares to blanks on the 6, he's assured his partner of playing the ⬜ 🁢 (since the next player can't cover both blanks in one turn), setting up the door to the 4s.

Runt

The last player is often the most crucial of all, carrying heavy responsibility for the game strategy. First and foremost, he needs to make the lead player pass. Unless he can do this, the opponents will win.

To make the lead player pass, he needs to develop his strong suit, probably to a greater degree than the 3rd-lead needs to do so. He should attack by repeating and, if possible, squaring to his own strong suit, or to his partner's. This means he will probably pass up more opportunities to play his double tiles. For example:

After the leadoff with the 🁫, the 2nd-lead played the 🁡. The 3rd-lead played the 🁟, covering his partner's leading suit. Covering his partner's 6 tells us he probably doesn't have any 3s.

The runt may have the ⚂⚂ or the ⚀⚀, but he shouldn't play either if he has a better tile. If he has the ⚀⚂, then he should square to his partner's 3. This is such a straightforward play that, if he doesn't do it, it's assumed he doesn't have the ⚀⚂ in his hand. The second-best play he can do is to cover the 3rd-lead's 1 with a strong suit of his own. If he has no 1 tile that he considers strong, he may then double with the ⚀⚀. The ⚂⚂, being the double of the partner's strong suit, should be kept for later.

The runt should protect his partner against the attack of the lead player. His first play usually covers the leading double:

If he has any blanks, then he is expected to play one in order to cover the leadoff ▭, hopefully with a tile that will show his strong suit (and his double, if possible). If his hand has the following tiles:

his logical play would be the [1|6], since it both shows his double [6|6] as well as his strongest suit. He should *not* double with the [6|5], since this may allow the lead player to attack with the blanks (notice the [0|4] is missing and could be in the lead player's hand).

We now understand that the runt's main job in this first round is to cover the leadoff tile. This should be done even if the tile he plays is not a particularly strong one. If he doesn't cover it, then we can assume he has none of that suit. *Unless …*
Let's say that after a leadoff with the [0|1], the 2nd-lead thought for a long time before playing the [1|5]. This tells the runt that he needn't fear his partner will pass to blanks (since the 2nd-lead thought about it, he must have had a choice of tiles) and therefore shouldn't feel forced to cover the leadoff. It even makes him suspicious that the lead player may have led a bluff. In that case the runt should cover the 3rd-lead's tile with the strongest suit he has, attacking the lead player and keeping him off balance.

Just as the 3rd-lead tries to help the lead player develop his game, so should the runt be playing to thwart him. He should play tiles that won't allow the lead player to repeat his strong suit. He should also watch for signals in his partner's plays that tell him to take over the offensive of the game ("pull the hand"). The runt is often in a position to best guess the opponent's tiles, and can therefore win as often as (if not more than) his partner.

Pulling the Hand

The third and fourth positions, the "defensive players," are the most difficult ones to play well. These players are constantly balancing their need to discard bad tiles while developing their strong suits, with a mandate to help their teammates and thwart their opponents. They are the ones often asked to make sacrifices for the sake of their partners, such as not doubling when they can attack instead, or discarding doors they may hold in order to prevent their partners from passing or discarding their doors.

And all the time, like sharks circling bait, they need to be constantly looking for signs of weakness in their partners. To "pull the hand" means that the defensive player has decided his hand is the strongest and in the best position to win. He now plays tiles that benefit the development of his own game *at his partner's expense!*

If you believe your game is best, and are contemplating pulling the hand, keep the following points in mind. Unless your partner has clearly asked you to do so (by the way he's played so far), he is going to immediately feel betrayed. Even if you win, but especially if you lose the hand, you can expect at least some hard feelings on his part. Good manners dictate you should apologize to your partner at the end of the game, and explain why you thought you should play this way.

Here's an example of the runt (last player) pulling the hand:

Your partner is 2nd-lead and has played two 5s, the

[domino] and the [domino]. Clearly his strong suit showing is the 5. You have in your hand the [domino]. Although you played the first 6, as a supportive player you are expected to play this tile by squaring to 5s.

What would you do, however, if you also have in your hand the [domino] [domino] [domino]? If you were to square to 6s, there would be only one 6 missing (the [domino]), which someone would have to discard, and you'd keep all the remaining 6s. If you decide to pull the hand, you'd play the [domino] on your partner's 5 like this:

[row of dominoes]

You can also pull the hand by withholding your partner's strong suit, even though you're expected to develop it, simply because another play advances your own hand. This play might even be getting rid of a double tile. All "pulls" somehow involve subordinating your partner's game to yours.

What should you do if you're the partner whose hand has been pulled, even though you didn't want it to happen? If your partner's not prone to these exercises willy-nilly, then you need to trust his judgment. Re-examine the game played so far, in light of this new development. If it's the runt who pulled, he'll take care of making the lead player pass. Your job now is to make the 3rd-lead pass to help the runt take the lead.

If your team loses the game, then expect profuse apologies from the partner who pulled the hand and be sure to scold him, but only good-naturedly!

Building a House

So far we've been talking about strategy in a straightforward fashion. Even when pulling the hand, everyone could tell by your plays that you were doing so, and adjusted their strategy accordingly. It's all been very above-board and polite.

Now let's get dirty!

There is another way to develop your game that is not immediately obvious to the other players. It is called building a house. I think of it as a passive-aggressive strategy of play. If *we* compare what *we've* discussed before to an elegant fencing match, then this is more like mud wrestling: sneaky, controversial, ultimately rather selfish—but you might just win the bout.

Your leadoff was the after very little thought (which probably means you have good tiles in your hand—see page 81). The 2nd-lead plays the and your partner rapidly follows with the . This means your partner doesn't have any 1s to play and therefore was forced to cover your leading tile—right? And yet, if we take a look at his hand, this is what we find:

What's going on? Your partner decided that he had strong tiles and pulled the hand by *not* covering the 1. What's different about this "pull" compared to the ones discussed in the last chapter is that he is being sneaky about it. He needs more 1s, so he's trying to trick the opponents into playing them.

Building a house means you've decided your game isn't strong enough to attack, your partner's not worth supporting or defending, and you're looking for an alternative. So why not let the opponents help your game?

To do this you need to fool everyone else around the table *including your partner*. You must make the opponents believe that you are running away from a particular suit, when in reality you like it very much, in order to get them to develop it for you. Here's another example. You have the following hand:

and decide to lead with the .

Now you're in a position to cover either your own 5 or the runt's 2. The best reason to leave the 5 alone is because it was your lead suit and your partner expects you to protect it. The 2 was led by your opponent, so covering it with the ⬛ seems to be the right choice.

You have more 2s than 5s in your hand, however. It seems logical to try to develop the 2s. How can you do this? You could think for a while, then play the ⬛ rapidly to indicate you have no other 5s and decided to play with the 2s. Your partner now understands your strategy, but so do the opponents. It's unlikely that the runt will repeat a 2 when he realizes you want to play them. This may be the right time to build a house. Think before playing the ⬛, then play it at normal speed. A frown as you think may not be a bad idea. If another player is watching your expressions, he'll surmise that covering your own lead tile is distasteful to you. Everyone will assume you have no 2s, and at least one other 5, and you only grudgingly played the ⬛.

Now the fun begins. If your opponents take the bait, they will repeat the 2 as soon as possible and prevent the 5s from being developed—falling right into your trap. Later in the game, when the truth comes out, the opponents will be demoralized as they realize they've been had.

Such a sneaky play is a calculated risk. You can't expect much help from your partner, since he's not clear on what your game is. You now depend upon the opponents' plays. You can't build a house too often, or your opponents will quickly wise up to you. Worse yet, you may lose your partner's support. The common phrase an upset partner exclaims is "I'm playing against two enemies and a traitor!"

And yet, sometimes you just have to cut loose— go wild—play it *unsafe* and add some spice to your game-playing. Just be prepared to pay the possible consequences.

How to Locate the Unplayed Tiles

Several times in this book there's been a statement like "… if you think the opponent's strong suit is the 5," or "… since your partner has no 3s." How are you supposed to know these things?

Figuring out the tiles in the other players' hands is an advanced skill that requires most of the concepts we've been discussing in the prior chapters. Above all, it requires a keen memory, in order to be able to recall the plays made. I recommend very strongly that you develop this ability to remember by practicing the memory exercises presented in "Mental Exercises" (page 50).

For the sake of the subsequent discussion, let's assume you've been playing for a while and have the basic skills down pat. You are now able to reconstruct most of the skeleton as it's been played (who played what tile, and under what circumstances).

You only know *for sure* seven tiles at the beginning of a game: those in your hand. As tiles are played, there will be fewer and fewer unplayed ones to guess, so it becomes easier to figure them out. The goal, which is not always achieved, is to be able to identify them by the time each player has only two tiles left in his hand.

At the beginning of the game you don't know the other 21 tiles. You will make tentative guesses on what the other players have by the way they play. Remember that you may be playing with others who may not follow your strategy, or just don't know how to play well, so their plays may confuse you. But there is one way you can learn about their tiles that is 100% for certain: their passes.

If a player passes to a certain suit, you can now disregard all seven tiles of that suit from his hand. Eliminating these tiles makes your guessing a lot easier.

Consider the problem opposite: you led with the ![domino], and later passed more than the other players. Now all others have one tile left to play, while you have two. You can play either the ![domino] or the ![domino]. If you knew the other players' tiles, you could make sure your partner wins.

What are the three unplayed mystery tiles? You should be able to tell by studying the skeleton.

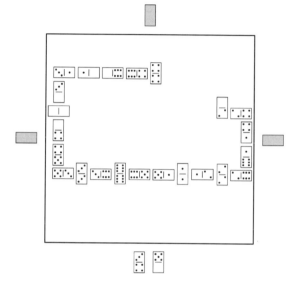

Yes, you're correct: they are the , the and the . If you had to guess, you'd have a one-third chance of guessing right and making the winning play.

You recall the first few tiles played and see that after the 2nd-lead played the , your partner played the [5-1]; he didn't double on the 5! You should therefore expect him *not* to have the [5-5]. Good! Now guessing will get you fifty-fifty odds.

But you also realize that the 2nd-lead played as his first tile the 5, and your partner seemed to shy away from it the second time it was played, so the 5 is probably the opponents' strong suit. Although it may still be a guess, your partner probably has the [2-1] and you should play the [3-2].

If you recall your partner passed to 5s, would that make it any easier? Of course—now you're sure about his tile, since you can identify it as the only non-5, the [2-1]. Playing the [3-2] is a guaranteed win.

Apart from the passes, all other ways to figure out the tiles are not as clear-cut. The passes only tell you what the player doesn't have; you'll have to discover what he actually has by the way he plays.

Although the opponents would like to hide their game from you, they must still try to communicate between themselves. If you follow their plays, they often can't help but declare their hands. Here's an example: You're the lead player and you lead with the [•|•]:

[domino] [domino] | [domino] [domino]

After this round you should know that your partner (3rd-lead) doesn't have the [domino] and, since he played the [domino], his strong suit might be the 2s.

[domino] [domino] | [domino] [domino] [domino] [domino]

The runt played the [•|••] and you doubled up on it. The 2nd-lead squared to his partner's 5 with the [domino] and your partner played the [domino], repeating the opponent's 4. This is not a play you would expect him to make, since you're not supposed to develop the opponent's suit (Second Law). This probably means he has no other 5s.

You also keep in mind that the 2nd-lead didn't like the 2, since he squared against it, so he probably has few or no others. It would seem like a good idea to help your partner develop his 2s.

It's important to figure out the other players' strategies, or styles of play, in order to guess at their tiles. This is not too hard to do if you know the people you're playing with. If they're strangers, however, it'll probably take you a few games into the match before you can figure them out. I make guesses as to their tiles, and then observe what they play. As the game progresses and their tiles get played, I learn what they *really* had in their hands. In this fashion I can determine their skill level and strategy of the game.

Do they play primarily so as not to yield suits? Do they like to build houses? These styles of play make it very difficult to figure out their tiles. That is why sometimes beginner players may defeat an experienced team. Long-term, though, playing in a nonlogical way doesn't lead to consistent victories, since not even your partner can figure out what your hand is nor help you develop it.

If the opponents are experienced, then I assume that they're playing the best they can with whatever tiles they have, and that they'll be following the Three Laws of Dominotics. I assume that they will first attack, if possible, with their strong suit. Next I assume they'll take any good chance they have to cover, repeat, and square. If they don't do so, then it's either because they're concerned over a double tile, or they just don't have the appropriate tile. Finally, if they cover their own strong suit, or their partner's, then it's because they don't have a tile for the other side of the skeleton—or they have what would be a terrible one to play (the opponent's door, for example).

These assumptions may not be correct, though. The player may not have recognized a key play, and therefore may not have made it. He could also be intentionally trying to confuse you. He may even simply make a mistake in his tile choice.

In summary, when you try to guess the other players' tiles, always think about the following four points:

1. The only tiles you know for sure are those in your own hand.

2. Remember the passes, as this is the only 100%

assured knowledge you have about the others' tiles; namely, what they don't have.

3. Determine what strategy of play the others follow.

4. If the others are experienced, then observe the plays they make—and realize the ones they might have done, but didn't. Assume that if they didn't play a particular tile that would have been to their advantage, then it's because they don't have it. You will have the best chance to locate the tiles by eliminating possibilities and by making informed guesses according to those played.

The Jam

The jam is a play that terminates the game being played. It happens when a tile is used to square to a suit so that all seven tiles of that particular suit are played. No further play is therefore possible. The unplayed tiles in each team are then put together and their points are added. The team with the fewest points gets the total points of *both* teams.

If the total points of one team equals the total of the other team, the jam is deemed a tie and the game is played over. The player who originally led off that game gets to lead off again.

What is the importance of a jam? With this one play you directly control the fate of the game. In one stroke you can win big—or lose big. The stakes are also higher: the points earned are usually more than what you earn when a game ends by discarding the last tile (dominating). This is generally true, even though the most points you can possibly win by dominating is 129, and the highest jam can only give you 126 points.

Psychologically, this play can be a traumatic experience. While the person who has the "jamming tile" (JT) is pondering his choice, all you can do is wait and hope he'll make the decision that will benefit you. You also try to develop a poker face so he won't see your barely suppressed joy (or dread) at the thought of the coming jam.

This play is sometimes the only way out of a hopeless situation. You may have a hung double tile and can't win by dominating—but still might win by jamming the game (a ⬚ or a ⬚ are great tiles to have in a jam). You may even be about to lose the game and are desperately hoping a jam will result in a tie, thus giving you an opportunity to play the game over without a penalty.

How can you tell if a jam is a right choice to

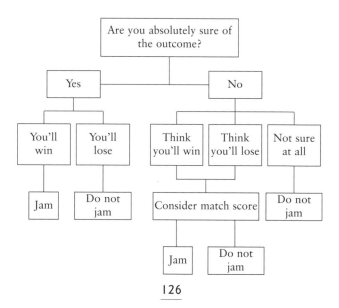

make? The first task you have to do is to figure out how many points are unplayed. You add the points of the tiles played (*including* the points of the JT about to be played) and subtract them from 168 (the total number of points of all 28 tiles). Then you may follow the decision tree opposite.

The first decision branch in this tree is to determine if you can be absolutely sure you'll win or lose the jam. How is this possible? Observe the example on the next page.

You have the jamming tile (JT), the ⚅⚃. First you add all the played points, which equal 97. Add those of the JT and you have a total of 104. Now subtract 168 − 104 = 64 points in the unplayed tiles. This means if you and your teammate have total points less than 32, you win the jam.

Your own tiles (after you play the JT) add up to 2 points. Now assuming your partner has the three heaviest tiles (the ones worth the most points), how much would he have? The three unplayed tiles with the most points are ⚅⚅, ⚅⚅, and ⚅⚅ (tied with ⚅⚅), which total 27. If you now add your own points, you see your team can have *at most* 29 points. This is a jam you can't lose. Play the ⚅ on the ⚅.

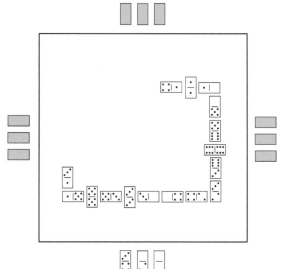

For another result, consider the example opposite. There, your jamming tile is the ⚅. The total of played points, *including* the JT, is 140. There are therefore 28 points unplayed, and 14 are needed for a tie. If you assume your partner has the three lightest tiles, the █·1█, the █·1·█, and the █:·1█, he would have 7 points. This, added to your █:·1·█, is 15 points. Since the fewest number of points your team can have is more than half of the unplayed points, you can't win the jam. So play the █:·:·█ on the 5 and let the game continue.

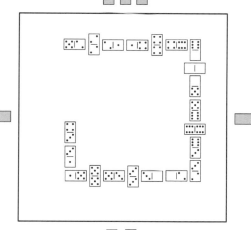

As you've seen, adding up the points can give you critical information, so it's important to be accurate in your calculations. This is a good time to give you a hint: in a jamming situation, the total of the unplayed points (after you play the JT) *must always be an even number*. If your calculations give you an odd number, go back and add again.

The next branch in the decision tree to consider is what to do if you can't be absolutely sure you'll win the jam. You may have one of three impressions: you suspect your team has fewer points and will therefore win, you suspect your team will lose, or you have no idea who will win.

Perhaps the easiest one to deal with is what to do if you have no idea at all. Usually this is because the jam has come early in the game, before you've had a chance to figure out the other players' tiles. This also means there are probably a lot of points out there to be won—or lost! Jamming the game in this situation is pure gambling, and you must decide if you're a gambler at heart or not. I usually don't jam when faced with this situation.

It is difficult to know what to do when you're somewhere in between being certain of the outcome of a jam and having no idea at all, but this is actually the most common situation you'll find yourself in. By then, you've begun to guess the other players' tiles and have a fighting chance of predicting the outcome. Consider the example below.

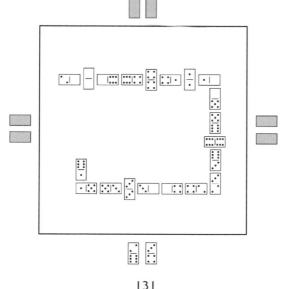

The JT is the ⚅⚀. Now the total of unplayed points is 44, and there is no 100% assurance of either losing or winning. I'll let you do the calculations, but your team can have a maximum of 26 points (more than half of points left—you lose) or a minimum of 14 (you win).

It might seem like the outcome is now left to chance, until you remember (in this sample game) that the opponents were playing the 5s as their strong suit. Your partner didn't double on the 5, but rather covered it, so he probably doesn't have the ⚄⚄. Assume therefore he has only one 5, the heaviest one being the ⚅⚄. Now assume his other tile is the heaviest non-5 left (the ⚅⚀ or the ⚅⚁), and when you add his 13 to your 7 points, you get only 20 points. You should win the jam, 20 points to 24.

Otherwise, if it's your partner who has been playing the 5s, then assume he has two of the three left. If he has the two lightest ones, he has a total of 16 points (the ⚄⚄ and the ⚄⚅), and with your 7 you get 23 and you lose the jam.

132

There will still be situations where you may not know the right choice to make. You may think you'll win, but can't be sure, and worry about the consequences that losing the jam will have on the match. This is when I recommend figuring the match score into your calculations.

You will probably feel more brave and jam the game if it's early in the match, or if the opponents have few total points. This way, if you lose, you still have plenty of opportunities to make up for your mistake. You will, however, be reluctant to jam if all they need to win are the points at stake. It's better in that case to open the game and dump points, hoping to win the next game.

Sometimes your partner can give you a hint that he thinks a jam would be good, and this hint may tip the scales one way or the other. You may see your partner think long and hard when he knows you have the JT, and then very deliberately play a tile so you get a chance to jam the game. This means he has studied his hand, determined it's not too heavy, and wants to give you the signal that it's okay by him to jam. This is called "asking for the jam." Now you can study your own tiles and let them make the decision for you.

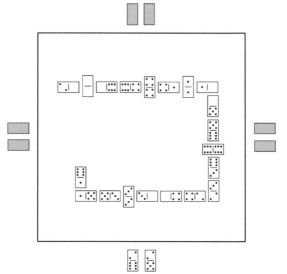

It's been said that it's not wise to jam a game that's already won, as in the example above.

You have the 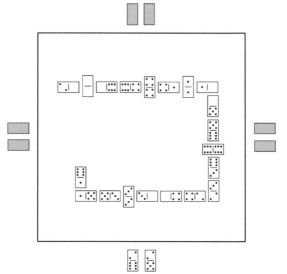, but this time you also have another 2 and are therefore not obligated to play the JT. When you add the points and calculate, you realize that the outcome is not absolutely known (if your partner has heavy tiles, you lose the jam). You also realize that if you play the 🁣, then no one can stop you from winning by discarding the 🁫 in the next turn because *you* are the lead player at this point. Why then run the risk of jamming the game?

This reasoning is a sound one *if* you're not sure who would win the jam, or if you think you'd lose it. If you're pretty sure you'd win it, however, then *not* jamming is foolish. All you're doing is allowing the opponents to discard tiles, whose points would have been added to your team score.

Even with a won game, therefore, seriously study the possibility of the jam. It may be worth it.

What if you don't jam the game? Perhaps you have another tile that can play instead of the JT (as in the last example), and may therefore keep the door for at least one more round. If you don't have such a tile then your only other choice is to square to the other number.

If I'm your partner and I see you do this, then I should understand that you were afraid of losing the jam. Is this because you think I have heavy tiles, or are *you* the one who's loaded with points? The answer to this question will tell me a lot about your hand. It is unlikely you have any others of the suit you squared to; otherwise you would have played another tile and kept the JT.

Talking about the jam can be an exhaustive task—and yet there may always remain an element of uncertainty in your decision of whether to do it or not. Unless the outcome is a sure thing, the jam will always remain, in a sense, a calculated gamble, a gamble that may significantly advance your game—or sink it!

The Three Doors (and Other Stories)

In this chapter I've collected a few plays and situations that couldn't be clearly pigeon-holed into one category or another. Let's discuss them one at a time.

The Three Doors

Let's say that a square has happened so you are left holding the last two doors and the double. See the example on the next page.

You're the lead player now. What could be easier than to double with the ⬛, make everyone pass, and then play either door?

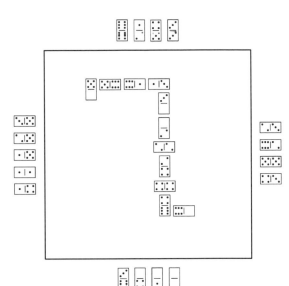

As in this example, it often happens that after you follow up with one of the doors, on the next round you'll have to discard the last one and you'll lose the game! Try to play either the [image: 1 3] or the [image: 1 1] and you'll see what I mean.

It is therefore better to hold on to that double. This way, when the runt plays the [image: domino] or the

⚀⚃ (depending on which blank you play) you'll be able to double with the [⚀] and still hold on to the door. When your partner sees you play your double, he'll know what suit you don't have and will try to protect you from it.

Keeping the double tile effectively gives you two doors in a row. So why would you ever want to play the double? I can think of only one good reason: if your three doors are your last three tiles. In that case, play the [⚀] to make everyone pass and proceed to dominate the game.

The Open Tile

Your partner has just led with an open tile; that is, a tile that has a different suit on each side and is therefore not a double. There are several different strategies to follow, according to what you think is going on.

Almodovar's Opening

⚅⚁ ⚃⚁

Your partner leads with the ⚃⚁ and you observe you have neither of the doubles. You start suspecting he used Almodovar's Opening. If so, your partner probably has a poor game with many doubles, and led with an open tile whose suit's doubles are in his hand (he has the ⚃⚃ and the ⚁⚁). When the 2nd-lead doesn't double either, then it's almost assured your assessment is correct, since it's unlikely the runt has both doubles.

What you should do is immediately square to the 6, since this will help your partner play the ⚃⚃. If you don't do so, it's assumed you don't have the ⚀⚃.

The 2nd-Lead Doubles

You immediately know this is not Almodovar's, since the 2nd-lead played a double. You may even have the other double in your hand. What should you play?

If you have the ![domino], then this should be the obligatory play. With it, you won't be covering either of the leadoff suits, and you force the runt to play a fresh suit to your partner, who may then have the chance to square.

If you don't have the ![domino], then you need to play to cover the 6, so your partner knows you *don't* have the double and may therefore hang it if the opportunity presents itself.

The 2nd-Lead Covers and You Have a Double

![domino] ![domino]

You have the ![domino] or the ![domino], so you know this is not Almodovar's. You also may even have the ![domino]. What you *don't* want to do in this situation is to play a double, since it's possible that the runt may have the ![domino] and square to 4, perhaps making your partner pass and lose the lead. You would think for a while (if you have other 4s) then cover the 4 with an open tile. This keeps your partner out of trouble.

The Lead Player Has One of the Doubles

Let's say you have the ⚃⚃, so you know it's not Almodovar's. Yet on his next play, your partner doubles to the 6!

This means he felt secure enough his ⚅⚅ wouldn't be hung even if he led with the open tile—therefore he must have started with five or six 6s in his hand. Now you need to play in order to let him develop that monster suit.

It also tells us he has no 2s, otherwise he would have kept that ⚅⚅ in his hand.

The Ill-Repeat

As a corollary to cover, repeat, and square, there is a particular play that should be admonished: as a rule, you should not repeat the opponent's suit.

In this example you're the 3rd-lead. In the second round, rather than cover the 3 you played first, you played the ⚃. This helps to develop the opponent's suit (which is against the Second Law). At best, it may allow the opponent to double on the tile. At worst, being the third of that suit played, a square will give him the door(s).

It is therefore better to play something else rather than to repeat their suit. You may need to cover your partner's tile, or even your own, rather than assist in the development of the opponents' suit.

Perhaps the only time when the ill-repeat wouldn't be quite so dangerous is if you hold a door on the other side of the skeleton, and therefore know for certain that the opponents will have to cover the suit you play.

The Crossed Tiles

Let's say that during a game it becomes obvious that your team has a particular suit. One opponent may have passed to it and the other may have been forced to cover his own strong suit, or even thrown away a door. These are all clear signs that you and your partner have all the tiles left in that suit. For example:

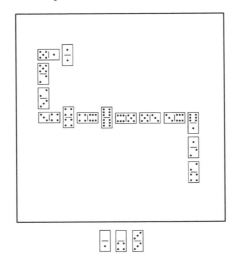

Your team's strong suit is the 1s. You have in your hand one of them, the [•|1]; you also have a 4, the [••|•]. You know for sure your partner has the other two 1s, the ⚄ and the ⚃. What do you play?

The answer would be very straightforward if you could square to the 1s, but you don't have the ⚄. Your first instinct might therefore be to leave the 1 alone, and cover the 4 with the ▦. Otherwise you'll be covering your strong suit, and may make your partner believe you have no 4s to play.

However, it often happens that whatever you play on the 4 can be used by your next opponent to attack your partner; he then has to cover the 1 with one of his tiles, such as the ⚃. This leaves each of you with one 1 in your hand and, because you *didn't* square to 1, the ⚄ is now known to be in your partner's hand.

Having crossed tiles (one in each teammate's hand) is troublesome. The opponents can now play their tiles so that neither of you can play the 1; they'll play blanks to him, and 4s to you. It's often therefore much more powerful to cover the 1 with the ▪, but *only* if you're sure your partner has the other two 1s.

Consider thinking for a while before playing the ⬜. Your partner, who knows you have only one 1, should understand you do have a 4, but decided not to cross the strong suit. The opponents may be fooled into thinking not only that you have no 4s, but also that you have other 1s. They won't expect your partner to have both of them, and this may even allow a jam to be set up since they may not expect him to have the JT.

As an aside, what if you did have the ⬜ in your hand? You should square to 1s, make the opponent pass, and your partner should then play his tile *rapidly*. He won't fool you, since you know he has the door, but the opponents may be tricked into thinking you have it—and inadvertently allow your partner to jam the game.

The Last Door

Your partner has just now been forced to discard his door, and never had a chance to contemplate a jam. Now it's your turn to play and you're desperately trying to figure out what his remaining tile is—but you have *absolutely no idea!* What do you do?

I always depend on figuring out the tiles, rather than relying on luck or hunches. But there's a "rule" that has helped me often in this situation. Consider this:

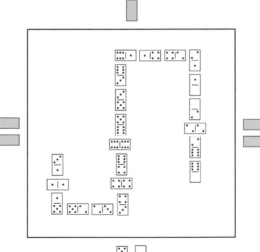

The door your partner played was the ⬛. If he had been presented with a blank before, he would have attacked with the ⬛. He may have even considered jamming the game, if it happened to be the jamming tile. This means he was most likely never given the chance to play a blank—and therefore it is likely he has another blank in his hand.

You can reconstruct the skeleton in your mind (you've been practicing, haven't you?), and can determine for a fact if your partner did indeed have a chance to play a blank. When you don't know for sure what your partner's tile is, and feel the need to guess, look at the other suit on the door he just discarded and assume he has one of those left. In this case, squaring to blank with the ⬛ may be your best chance to win this game, since now there's a blank on either end of the skeleton, assuring one for your partner.

The Penultimate Sacrifice

If the ultimate sacrifice is to hang your own double to benefit your partner, then the penultimate one must be to throw away your door when you're not forced to. The sacrificial player is the one that has more tiles, trying to prevent his leading partner from passing.

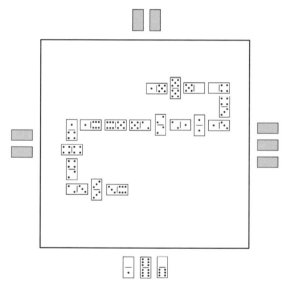

It's your turn, and what could be more clear-cut that your need to double with the 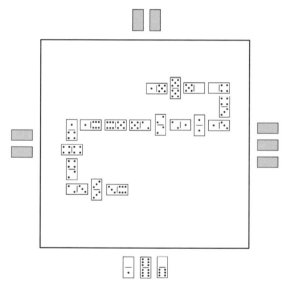? After all, you discard a bad tile and still retain the door to the 1s. You fleetingly remember your partner led with the , but fail to grasp that clue's significance.

So you play the and promptly proceed to lose the game. What happened? Here's how the tiles were actually distributed:

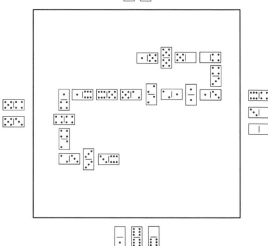

If you'd been following the game and trying to guess the tiles as you went along, then this shouldn't have been a surprise to you. Any play other than to sacrifice your door causes your partner to pass and the opponents to win.

Your partner led with the [2|2] and played to develop this suit. Observing that the two 2s left were the [5|2] and the [3|2], you realize that playing the [1|2] door ensures one of them can be played and opens up the game for your partner. You should think before playing it, though, so he realizes you weren't forced into it and therefore still had another play option.

Man Overboard!

The lead player leads with the [4|5] and your partner passes right off the bat. The 3rd-lead plays the [4|3] and it's your turn to play the runt position. If you have options on both sides of the skeleton, what do you do now? Do you cover the 4 to help your partner (throw a line to the man overboard)? Or, since he already passed, do you hoard the 4 in your hand to have when you're next attacked with it (let him sink or swim)?

These are the facts: 1) You need to make both the lead player and the 3rd-lead pass if you hope to win; and 2) you need your partner's help to do this. How can he make an opponent pass when he's drowning against the 4s? Let's look at the different possibilities.

If you have the double of the tile shown by the 3rd-lead (in this example the [⋰⋱]), then you should play it. You get rid of a double and you force the lead player to cover either his partner's or his own suit. Either way, your partner should be able to play on his next turn.

If you don't have that particular double and you have one or two 4s, then you should cover the 4. This ensures that the lead player can't repeat the 4 and your partner should be able to play.

What if you have three or four 4s—should you sneakily leave the [⋰⋱] alone in order to build a house and try to win with them? It is sometimes said, "He who plays with the lead amuses himself but doesn't win!" Unless you have an overwhelming group of tiles, it's still better to cover the 4 and help your partner.

What if you have only one 4—and the other side of the tile is also the only one of its suit? For example, your only 4 is the ⚃⚄—and it's also the only 5 you have. Playing it might be counterproductive, since you yield both suits in one fell swoop. You may also make your partner wrongly believe that the 5s are your strong suit, and he might play to develop them. On the other hand, keeping this tile is very dangerous because you may be forced to play it on a 5. It's best to throw a line to the man overboard. Play the ⚃⚄ quickly, so your partner knows it's the only 4 you have, and he might therefore be suspicious of the 5s.

If you have *five* 4s in your hand, though … beware everyone. You're pulling this hand!

The Betrayal

You are the 3rd-lead and you have these tiles:

The standard play is to cover the opponent's blank with the ⟦ⁱ•⟧. Some influential players have advocated the ⟦•∷⟧ (covering your partner's leadoff tile) as a reasonable alternative play. Let's see if we can understand why.

Both of the tiles already played are low in points. There's a chance your partner might be thinking of jamming the game if he's playing the 1s, and he must somehow find out you are loaded with points. Playing the ⟦•∷⟧ shows the 5s as your strong suit, as well as the double in your hand, and begins to discard points. If your partner helps you by repeating the 5 (as he should) you are now in a very strong position to dominate the game. If you also happen to jam with your 5s, the 1s in your partner's hand are now an asset.

Remember to think before *rapidly* playing the ⚀⚄. This will clearly tell your partner you do have a blank but chose not to use it, and that this was your only 1. You now hope the betrayal will be understood for the smart play it can be.

Sample Games

The four sample games presented here illustrate the concepts taught throughout the book. These games are seen exclusively from my point of view; you won't know what the other players' tiles are until they lay them down.

My playing technique is similar to that of chess: there are only a limited number of plays possible, which I constantly try to anticipate. While the players think, I ask myself what will be the tile played and what will be the consequences following its play. If I think far enough ahead, then I'll know what my best play should be when my turn comes up. In this way I'll be able to play fast or slow (in order to use thinking to communicate with my partner) without having to waste time and possibly confuse my partner.

I start each game by analyzing my hand and deciding what will be my initial strategy (offensive, defensive, or supportive). Next I try to figure out the other players' strategies as well as their strengths and weaknesses, according to the tiles played. I keep track of the doubles and make guesses about the location of unplayed tiles. The Three Laws of Dominotics are always kept in mind.

To get the most out of these examples you should follow along with your domino set. Start by separating the seven tiles I begin with, and leave the rest in a separate pool from which you will draw as needed to build the skeleton. After each game is done, you should be able to figure out the tiles that the other players started with. You may wish to distribute them and replay the game to better follow my observations and suggestions. I will be the South player, playing with North against East-West.

Game in Which I Play the Lead Player Position

My hand is this:

It is a poor hand because I have three doubles and no blanks. Since I have more than two doubles, I look for a tile that would allow me to lead off with Almodovar's Opening. I find the .

After thinking awhile (letting my partner know I'm having trouble deciding what to play) I lead the . East thinks for a while, then plays the . My partner has figured out why I led with the , and assumes I have the and . My partner squares to 5 with the . It's a good play because he's repeating the 5 and allows me to double.

West thinks a disturbingly long time (he has many 5s), then plays the .

Here's the blank I was dreading! At least I get to

play my 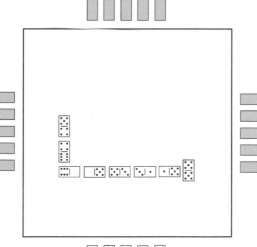. East also thinks for a while, then plays the ⬚. If he covers his partner's blank he either has no 5s or needs to develop the 6s. My partner plays the ⬚ without thinking about it too much. Is that his only 6? Apparently he doesn't have the ⬚. Surprisingly, West then squares to 5 with the ⬚, trying to wrest control of the 5s.

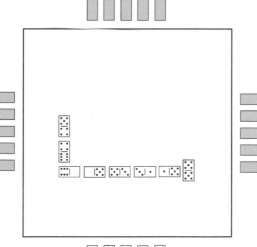

I pass—but so do East and North! This is called a general pass and the two remaining 5s are in West's hand. West has now gone from last position to first, from runt to lead player. He smiles, then plays the , repeating his partner's 6.

Now I have a choice on the 6s. I won't play the , because then I'd be repeating the 1 that East played first. I therefore play the , 2s being my strongest suit. East rapidly plays the  (no other 2s?). My partner again thinks on the 1 and, after deliberating, doubles with the . West plays the , repeating his blank.

I pass. Couldn't my partner have prevented the blank from being repeated? Since I have the , the other 1 left (which must be in North's hand,

160

since he thought on it) is the ⟨•⃞••⟩, and the ⟨••⃞•⟩ is also unplayed. A blank may have been unavoidable.

Now East stops and thinks for a while. Can we figure out what his blanks are? It's not the ⟨ ⃞1⟩, or he would have doubled as his second move. It shouldn't be the ⟨ 1•⟩, since he played his 2 last turn rapidly. This leaves us with the ⟨ 1•⟩ and the ⟨ •••⟩, and we understand his dilemma.

He doesn't want to play the 3, since it's my leadoff. He's unhappy about the 4 because my partner played one already. He finally decides to play the ⟨ •••⟩, perhaps as the lesser of two evils.

Now my partner thinks a relatively long time (he has a choice of 4s), then doubles with the ⟨••••••⟩ … and West loses his door to the 5s!

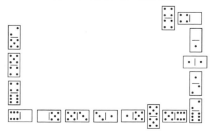

My partner is strong in 4s. I have the 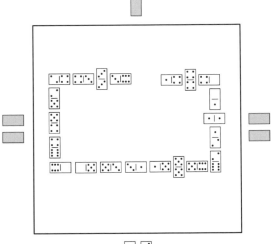 and I square to 4. East passes! My partner (North) now thinks for a short while, then plays the ⸱⸱⸱⸱ to repeat my leadoff. He well knows that I have the ⸱⸱⸱⸱. West passes (no 3s and my partner has the door to 4s), and North becomes the lead player.

Now I get to play my 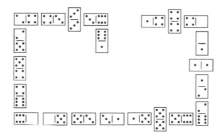. East thinks about it briefly, then plays the domino, repeating his 6. My partner indeed has to discard his door, the domino. West passes again.

Now I have the choice of either jamming the game to 1, hanging the domino, or squaring to 6 and letting East jam. Do you agree that East has the domino? There should be no doubt about that. West just passed to 6 and North threw away his door to 4s because of the 6.

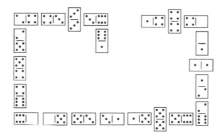

Can I win the jam to 1? After jamming there will be 142 points played, so 26 points are still unplayed. Half of that is 13, so we win if the opponents have more than that. The three smallest unplayed tiles are the [1], the [2-1], and the [3-1]. Added to the [6-6], this makes a *minimum* possible of 17 points for East-West, so this is a jam I cannot lose!

East had the [2-1] along with the [6-6], while North had the [3-2]. Our team wins the jam's 26 points.

Game in Which I Play the 2nd-Lead (West Leads)

My hand is this:

[1-0] [3-3] [4-4] [5-3] [6-1] [6-4] [6-2]

It is an average hand, lacking 2s and having one double with another of its suit. The 6s are my strongest suit with three of them. I'm already worrying that West may lead with the [5-3], because then I'll pass immediately.

The leadoff, however, is the [5-4]. This means either a terrific hand for West (no doubles) or perhaps an Almodovar's Opening, since I don't have either double. I play the 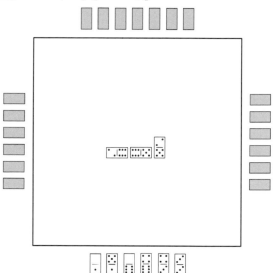, to show my partner my best suit. East squares to 2 with the ▦. North, my partner, passes.

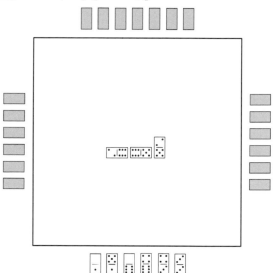

Disaster! The opponents have all the 2s! And now, if West has the ▦, he will play it and make me pass. If he does have it, then it's likely he started with five 2s in his hand. He plays the ▦, however. That means I've now located the [⚄:⚀] in East's hand.

I can now play the [⚅:⚅] or the [⚅:⚄]. If I play the double, then the next player can't square to 2 and therefore my partner should be able to play. The 2s, however, are unstoppable, and if we're going to have a chance of winning this game then they must be spent quickly. The [⚅:⚄] may be a better play. Besides, the [⚃:⚁] may not be in East's hand, and this way I'd locate another tile. Even if East squares to 2 and my partner passes again, West would still be unable to make me pass. I therefore play the [⚅:⚄].

East had the right tile after all and plays the [⚃:⚁], making my partner pass again.

West has to cover another of his 2s and therefore can't threaten me. He thinks for a short time, then plays the [⚁:⚀]. If he thought about it, then he probably has the other 2 in his hand, the [⚁:⚁].

166

Now my choices are the [1-5] or the [1-0]. I've already figured out the [2-0] is in West's hand, so if I play the blank, East can't square to 2s again. If I play the [1-5], then I'm playing the other lead suit, helping to develop the 5s. The choice is clear: I'll play the [1-0].

Consider that if West thought on the 2 without having any others, then East has the [2-0] and I've fallen into a trap, giving him the chance to jam the game, which would be a huge loss for my team.

East rapidly plays the [2-2]. He not only hasn't the door of the 2s, he probably has no blanks in his hand.

Now it's North's first chance to play. He thinks for a while, so he has other blanks. The best play to make is the [6-0], to repeat my 6, but I have that tile. A bad play would be to double on the blank (allowing a jam) or play a 5 (which West led). A [1-0] or [1-2] would be a good tile, if he has either of them. He plays the [1-0].

West, still the lead player, plays the [2-5]. This is a good play since he repeats his other lead suit, the 5s.

My play is forced: the ⟨dominoe⟩. East plays the ⟨dominoe⟩, clearing his double.

The best play for North now to make would be to repeat the 3, if he has the ⟨dominoe⟩. This would not only be a repeat to West, it might allow me to play my ⟨dominoe⟩. Of course, he doesn't know who has the ⟨dominoe⟩, just that West doesn't have it (he would have led the game with it, or played it in the last round). He thinks for a short while, then plays

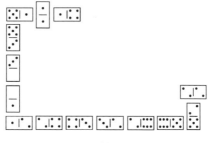

the [1|4]. Is it because he doesn't have the [1|6]? After all, the [2|6] is missing and East might attack with it. Does my partner have the [2|6] and therefore know West can't play it? Or was he simply trying to repeat the 4, which was my second tile played?

West now doubles with the [4|4]. If he led the game with an open tile, then this means he probably has no other 4s. This is critical information. He now has two tiles left and we know one is the [1|0] and the other one is *not* a 4. This other tile could be a 6 or a blank but if it's a 5 (his other lead suit), then it has to be the [2|0]. I have now tentatively guessed his remaining tiles.

Although my play is forced, the [4|6] is still a strong play. I'm repeating the 6 that I started with, and the [3|0] is in my hand so West won't get the blank he needs to jam the game.

East rapidly plays the [3|1]. He doesn't have the [3|6], which must therefore be in the hand of my partner, and by the quickness of his play it seems like he has no other 6s.

North plays the 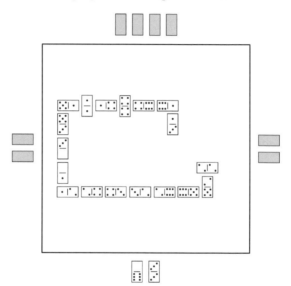. He did have it after all! I wish he had played it during his last turn.

Can we figure out the tiles in the other players' hands? Let's start with East. We already know he has no blanks, and if we also eliminate the 6s, then the only two tiles left are the and the .

West has the door of the 2 and, I think, the **[6–2]**. This is purely a guess, though. In that case my partner must have the **[6–6]** and the **[6–5]** in his hand, as well as the **[6–2]** and the **[0–1]**.

Now I've tentatively figured out everyone's tiles using the observations and assumptions made throughout the entire game. Let's see if the subsequent plays prove me right. To begin with, West shouldn't have a 3 and he should be forced to discard his door. Sure enough, he plays the **[0–2]**. The 2s are finally dead.

My **[6–1]** is in danger of getting hung, but what would happen if I doubled with it? East would pass (no 3s or blanks). North would then need to make a decision. Should he play his **[6–6]** in order to send me the 6 that I need? This would leave the blank open and I think that West has a blank and would win. The same would happen if my partner doubled with the **[0–0]**. If he covered the blank with the **[0–6]** then both West and I would pass, but East would play the **[6–6]**, and West would win with his **[6–1]**.

171

My other choice would be to play the 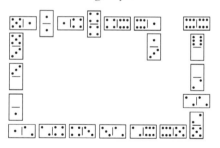, sending the 6s to my partner. East would pass and my partner should realize that I have the 1/1 (and *not* hang it). The best play to make then would be to hang his own 6/6 by squaring to 3, giving me the win and keeping the 6/6 to count as points for us. Will he understand what I'm trying to do?

I play the , and East passes. North, not being too sure of himself, decides to play the 6/6, keeping the door of the 6s—not the best play, but at least he doesn't hang my 3.

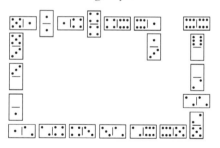

West passes! I win by playing my last tile, the 1/1.

Here's how the table looked at the end of the game:

It turned out that West had the ⬚ 1 ⬚, so although he did have a blank, I erred in the specific guess. Thankfully, it wasn't a critical mistake and the game played out to our advantage. Our team wins 37 points.

Game in Which I Play the 3rd-Lead (North Leads)

My hand is this:

There are no 6s and the only 2 is a double. I hope to combine either the 5s or the blanks with my partner.

North leads with the [4|4]. West quickly follows with the [4|6]. Since I have no 6s I must cover my partner's lead tile, and I play the [4|4] quickly to let him know I have no other 4s either. If East has the [4|6], then I would expect him to use it now. He indeed squares to 6s.

My partner rapidly plays the [5|6]. West thinks about it, then plays the [3|5], so he must have at least one other 3. I must double on the 2 because I have no other tile to play. I realize that the [3|6] is missing and East may have it, but I can do nothing to prevent the square. Bad luck: East has and plays it.

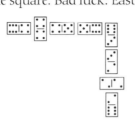

North passes this time. West now becomes the lead player and plays the 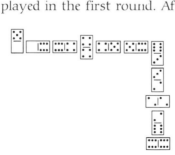 rapidly. Does this mean that East has the last two 6s left?

I take some time to think over the possible plays, and to let my partner know that I have several blanks. The strongest play seems to be to repeat the 5 that I played in the first round. After I play the

, East doubles with the . I take this to mean he has no 5s.

North now thinks a little and plays the . Doubling would have been a good play, so this means the is in West's hand and (since I have the) the other 5 in my partner's hand must be the . Observe, however, that the last 6 is the

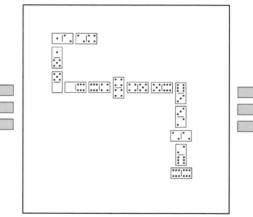

$\boxed{\cdot\ \vdots\vdots}$ and that if West has it he'll be able to jam the game. West plays the $\boxed{\cdot\ \vdots}$, however, so I suspect that East has the door.

I pass and the opponents now are the lead player as well as the 2nd-lead. East plays the $\boxed{\cdot\ \vdots\cdot}$. Repeating the opponent's suit is usually a poor play, but it's a good one in this situation since North will have to cover it.

North thinks and covers his lead suit with the $\boxed{\vdots\cdot\vdots\cdot}$, repeating the 1. West rapidly plays the $\boxed{\cdot\ \vdots\cdot}$. I think for a while (having two 3s) then play a devastating tile: the $\boxed{\vdots\cdot\vdots\vdots}$. If I've figured the tiles out correctly, East has no 5s and will lose his door, and North will have the opportunity to hang the $\boxed{\vdots\vdots\vdots\vdots}$. But will he? After all, he doesn't know that I don't have it, and he's seen me play three 5s. If he doesn't hang it, West plays it and we're dead.

But think further: The door to the 6s is the $\boxed{\vdots\vdots\cdot}$, and that will be the fifth 1 played. I have the last two 1s, so North will be forced to hang the $\boxed{\vdots\vdots\vdots\vdots}$! Sure enough, it all works out as expected.

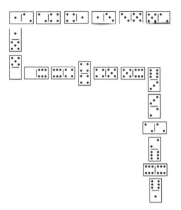

Although West remains the lead player, he's now unable to win because of his hung double. He plays the ⟦•⟧ and now I have a tough decision. I can jam the game by playing the ⟦ I• ⟧, causing a general pass, then playing the ⟦•I•⟧. The problem is that this is not a certain win. (I'll let you work out the details, but we could possibly lose the jam 16 points to 14.) I therefore decide to play the ⟦ I•• ⟧, repeating my partner's second suit played. East plays the ⟦•••••⟧ and North the ⟦•• I⟧.

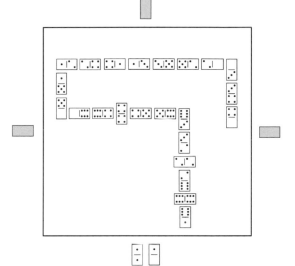

By now we know exactly who has what. North must have the 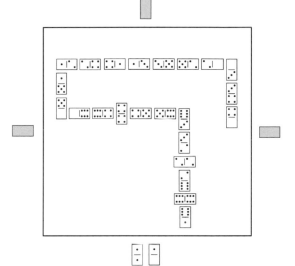, since East just hung it in the last round. West has the ⬛, and therefore East must have the ☐. After West passes, I win by squaring to 1 with the ☐ then dominating with the ☐.

Our team wins 16 points. It turns out I would have won the jam, but I'm not too disappointed with the final result.

Game in Which I Play the Runt (East Leads)

My hand is this:

It is not a great selection. Although I'm not lacking any suit, I have three doubles and no particularly strong suit. I am worried that the opponents may try to dominate us with the 3s, 2s, or 1s.

East leads with the [2|1]. My partner (North) plays the [2|6] rather rapidly. Bad news: He's weak in 2s. However, I'm glad to see that he played a 6, since I have two of them including the double.

West covers the 6 with the [6|5]. I play the [2|4] rapidly, to indicate this is my only 2.

East now repeats his 2 with the [2|2], a move that confirms their dominance of this suit. My partner

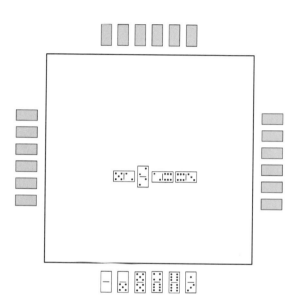

repeats the 6 with the ⬛. Yes! Let's see West cover that! He'll probably have to hit his partner's 2.

Contrary to my expectations he does cover the 6 with the ⬛. Now I'm getting very nervous as I contemplate my ⬛ possibly getting hung. I only have one possible play, the ⬛. Although this repeats West's 3, at least it prevents the 2 from being played. This play should also tell my partner that I don't have the [⠁|⠿] or else I'd play it now to repeat my 5.

[⠒⠄|⠁] [⠁|⠿] [⠿|⠿] [⠿|⠒] . [—] [⠁|⠿] [⠿|⠿] [⠿|⠒] [⠒|⠒] .

East, still the lead player, thinks for a while—then hits his 2 with the [⠒|⠄]. He must not have any 3s, since he had to cover his lead suit. And he probably has other blanks, since he chose to play one now.

Even better for us, the [|⠿] is somewhere out there, and my partner may now play it. He thinks for a long time. If he has this tile, then he's wondering if he should play it. After all, he doesn't know who has the other two 6s. He'll probably assume I have the [⠿|⠿], but what if East has the other one? Could the opponent be building a house with the 6?

North might also be thinking because he has the [⠒|⠒]. This is a good opportunity to discard this bad tile, but he may not get any other chance to attack with the 6 if he doesn't do it now.

Maybe he feels me across the table willing him to play it, because he ends up playing the [6].

Now West thinks a little. Perhaps he has the [2|2] and is wondering whether to double on the 3. If he does, however, he knows I might double on the 6, and his partner (having no 3s) will either pass or be forced to discard the door of the 6s (if he has it). He therefore dutifully covers the 3 and repeats his partner's blank with the [2|0].

Thanks to my partner's repeat, I have the two doors to the 6s. How can I make East pass? The [1] is probably a poor play, since we've already guessed he probably has at least one more blank and he won't pass to it. The [5|0] is a better play because I'm repeating my first suit, the 5.

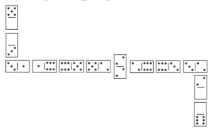

183

East passes. Now my partner is the new lead player, and he knows I have the last two doors to the 6s. He thinks on the 5 for quite a while, so he must have more than one 5. Let's try to figure out the possibilities. The [domino] wouldn't allow a 2 to be played, the others would. Does he have another 3? The [domino] comes to mind again. If he has it, it'll get hung if he plays the [domino].

After thinking, he plays the [domino]. He either can't stop a 2 from being played (having the [domino] and the [domino], and the last 2s being the [domino] and the [domino]), or he has the [domino] and is afraid of his [domino] getting hung. Perhaps he's really trying to get a 4 to me so I can jam the game ("asking for the jam").

West now plays the [domino], without much thought. Did he realize he was setting up a jam? Did he have any choice about it? He'd better *not* have the [domino], or his partner will kill him for not playing it!

Now I think about the jam. There are 110 points played after the game is jammed to 6s. The points in the hands are 168 − 110 = 58. To tie, our team must have 29 points. I have the 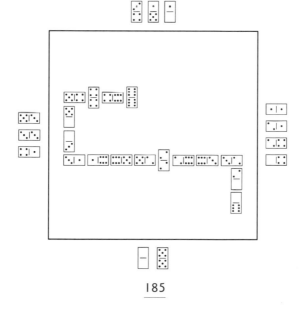 and the [I], for a total of 10 points. Can my partner have 19 points in his three remaining tiles?

We already figured out he has another 5. The highest one left is the (8 points), leaving 11 points in two tiles. The two highest tiles left are the and the , which would add up to 13 points. That means that the jam is not a sure win.

Let's also consider that on his third turn, when he played the [0|4], my partner thought about it. Did he have another blank? If he has just one blank we win the jam. Finally, keep in mind he did play the 4, almost as if asking for the jam. The decision is made.

The key plays here were all done by my partner. He played and repeated three 6s in a row, giving me the last two doors. Then he signaled a jam by playing the [3|3]. West made a big mistake, since he could have played the [5|1] instead of doubling with the [5|5] and letting me jam. Apparently doubling was too big of a temptation for him to resist, and he may have hoped the jamming tile was in my partner's hand.

We win the jam 24 points against their 34 points and add 58 to our total score.

Games for Two or More Players

BLOCKING GAMES

All of the games in this section have certain things in common: First, points are scored at the end of each hand, therefore there is no regard to the end count. Play is aimed, instead, at blocking your opponent from making a play. The game of Block and the game of Draw are two of the most simple and basic of all domino games. Many games are variations of one of these games. In both of these games, plays are made by matching suits with one of the tiles in your hand to one of the open ends in the line of play. The object of the game is to be the first player to domino.

The game of Block and the game of Draw are identical with one exception: In the game of Draw you draw extra dominoes from the boneyard if you are unable to make a play. In the game of Block you do *not* draw extra dominoes from the boneyard if you are unable to make a play. This seems to be the most widely used description of the difference between the game of Block and the game of Draw. However, in some places, the rules for a game called "Block" are that players draw from the boneyard when unable to make a play.

The game of Block is also known as Block Dominoes, the Block Game, and Allies (Block with Partners). The game of Draw also goes by the names Draw Dominoes, Draw Game, the Draw or Block Game, Block Dominoes with Buying, and even Domino Big Six, and Double-Six Dominoes.

The game of Doubles is sometimes called Maltese Cross. However, in all but one place, the rules I found to Maltese Cross did not contain the rule that makes Doubles a unique game: sometimes tiles cannot be played until the double of that suit has already been played. For that reason, I have listed these two games separately in this section.

Because all the games here are basically variations of Block, I have provided, under the heading "What's unique," details differentiating these Block games' variations from each other. Unless otherwise indicated, the following rules apply to each of the games below:

- One set of double-6 dominoes (28 pieces) is used.
- The dominoes are shuffled, facedown, at the beginning of each hand.
- The object of the game is to be the first player to domino.

Block

(aka Block Dominoes, the Block Game, and Allies)

Number of players: Best for 2 to 4 players.

Number of dominoes drawn: For 2 to 4 players, each player draws 7 tiles. If 5 or more are playing, prior to the start of the game players should determine and agree upon the number of tiles each player should draw from the deck. (If 2 players, each draws 7 or 8 tiles; 3 or 4 players, draw 5 or 6 tiles.)

If there are any remaining tiles after the draw, they are discarded, not used during that hand because there will be no drawing from the boneyard.

Set domino: Any domino may be used. Variations: (1) highest double, and in the event no double is drawn, reshuffle and redraw; (2) 6-6, and in the event the 6-6 is not drawn, reshuffle and redraw; or, (3) highest double, and in the event no double is drawn, play the highest single. After a tile has been set, play continues to the left.

How to play: Each player tries to match the pips on one end of a tile from his hand with the pips on an open end of any tile in the layout. If a player is unable to match a tile from his hand with a tile in the layout, the player passes his turn to the player on his left. Each player may play only one tile per turn.

The first player to get rid of all dominoes announces "Domino!" and wins the game. If none of the players can make a play, the game ends in a block. If a game ends in a block, all the players turn the tiles in their hands faceup, count the pips on each tile, and add them together. The player with the lowest total wins the game and earns the points (1 point per pip) of all the tiles left remaining in his opponents' hands. The player who first reaches 100 points or more is the overall winner.

Other rules: The game can be played with no spinners (which seems the most often used rule) or by using the first double as the only spinner of the game.

In most places, Block is played to 100 points. However, there are many different variations, including to 50, 150, 200, or 101 points.

Draw

(aka Draw Dominoes, the Draw Game, the Draw or Block Game, Block Dominoes with Buying, Domino Big Six, and Double-Six Dominoes)

Draw is the same as Block, with these exceptions:

After each player draws his hand from the deck, the remaining tiles are pushed to one side to make up the boneyard.

If a player cannot match a tile with one in the layout, he must draw from the boneyard until he picks a tile that can be played. He must keep the tiles he drew but couldn't use on that play. If there are no tiles left in the boneyard, the player passes his turn to the player on his left.

Mexican Train

(© 1994 by Roy and Katie Parsons)

Number of players/domino set: 2 to 4 players using the double-9 set (55 tiles); 5 to 8 players using the double-12 set (91 tiles). Adaptations can be easily made should your players/sets not exactly fit this guideline. Double-15 sets (136 tiles) can be used for even larger groups.

Additional equipment: A score sheet and one small marker per player (i.e., penny, dried bean, poker chip).

Object of the game: To rid your hand of as many dominoes as possible and to be the first to do this. The other players then must total the points or pips remaining in their hands and keep a running total for their score. The lowest score wins.

To begin, pull out the 12-12 if playing with a double-12 set (or the 9-9 if playing with a double-9 set) from the deck. This domino is called the "engine" and will be the centerpiece/starter for this game. Place the engine in the center of the table. Shuffle the remaining dominoes face down.

Number of tiles drawn: 2 players draw 12 tiles each; 3 players draw 11; 4 players draw 10; 5 players draw 12; 6 players draw 11; 7 players draw 10; and 8 players draw 9. Additional players can play by adjusting this numerical arrangement to fit.

Players draw their number of tiles with the

remaining tiles set aside in "bonepiles," to be drawn as needed later in the game.

The players then organize the tiles in their hands in a playable progression beginning with the same number as the engine/centerpiece. The tile ends must match and form a line to be ready to play as your "personal train" when the game starts (example: 12-5, 5-7, 7-8, 8-11, 11-1, 1-9, and so on). When you are no longer able to line up your tiles in a matching series, the leftover tiles are considered your "extras" and will be used on the

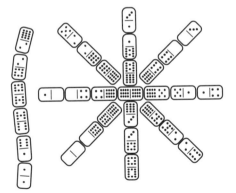

"Mexican Train" or on other players' "personal trains" during the game. If you do not draw a domino with an end that matches the engine/centerpiece tile, you can begin the line in your hand with any domino that will make up the longest line of end-matching tiles and the fewest "extras" possible.

To begin the game, choose a player at random to play first and then rotate the starters clockwise thereafter.

The first player must begin by either playing a matching tile from the "line-up" in his hand onto the engine/centerpiece nearest him, so beginning his "personal train," or by playing one of his "extra" dominoes to be the first of the Mexican Train. This Mexican Train is a line of "end-matching" dominoes that can run around the edge of the table or at some side space convenient to all players. The Mexican Train, one's own "personal train," and other players' "personal trains" (when markered) are the options that players can use to rid themselves of their tiles.

The Mexican Train begins with the first tile played by the player who chooses to play a domino from his "extras." It must be a domino whose end is the same as the engine/centerpiece. The train then grows as others play on it, but it can only be played on from the tail end, opposite the end that matches the engine's pips. The "personal trains" are spokes that grow outward from the engine/centerpiece and appear as spokes on a hub. Wooden or plastic hubs are available to conveniently hold the engine and the "personal trains." The number of spokes or "personal trains" coming from the engine are determined by the number of players participating. Spokes can be squeezed in, if more than 8 players are involved, or if double-15s are used.

It is always wise to start the Mexican Train as soon as possible as it gives more places to play. Try to play your "extra" tiles on the Mexican Train before you play on your "personal train."

After the starter has played one domino, the next player to the left does likewise by playing on the Mexican Train, beginning his own "personal train" leading off from the engine, or playing on another player's "personal train" if it has a marker on it. When a player cannot play on his own "personal train," or on the Mexican Train, or on another player's train, he must draw one tile and try to play it immediately. If unable to do so, the player passes and must put his marker out on the last tile in his "personal train" (even if it has not been started), marking it so that the last number to be matched shows clearly to everyone. Others can play indefinitely on that markered train until the "owner" plays on it and removes the marker.

If a player plays a double during play, it is placed sideways and he must then play a second domino somewhere on the table. He does not necessarily need to play on the double he has just played. If he cannot play a second domino, he must draw another tile, then either play it or place his marker on his personal train.

After a double is played, all play is delayed until someone can make a play on this double. It doesn't matter if the next player can play somewhere else or not. He must play a tile on the double tile, even if he has to play a tile out of his train line-up in his hand. (This is disrupting, but necessary.) If players cannot play a tile on the double tile, they must draw once. If they are still unable to play a tile on the double, they pass and must place their marker on their "personal train" even if they had a matching tile to play on their train before the double was played. This means that once a tile has been played on the double tile, anyone can play on any "personal train" that has a marker on it, although this can *really* disrupt that train for the owner.

A player can play two doubles, as long as that player is able to play an additional tile from his hand (he is not allowed to draw) on one of those double tiles. This means that a player could play three tiles in one turn.

Play then proceeds to the left. When any player is left with just one tile in his hand, he must give notice to the other players by tapping his final tile on the table. This allows other players a chance to lower their score by ridding themselves of a higher numbered tile on their next turn.

General rules: If a player has a tile in his hand that will play, he must play that tile. He may not draw another.

If there are no more tiles in the bonepile, a player must pass if he does not hold a playable tile.

It is possible for a game to end by playing a double alone and no one being able to play on it.

The game is over when one player has dominoed (played his final tile) or when the game is blocked because no one holds a playable tile. Then, all players must count the number of pips on the tiles left in their hands (0, in the case of the player who has dominoed), and give that number—their score—to the scorekeeper.

As soon as the first round is completed, the next game begins by pulling out the 11-11, if playing with a double-12 set, or the 8-8, if playing with a double-9 set. The starter tile is placed in the middle of the table for the engine, and the rest of the deck is shuffled before drawing hands. All "personal trains" and the Mexican Train must be started with this same numbered new tile. Each new game thereafter should begin with the next-lowest double being played as the engine, with the 0-0 tile being the final engine for the last game.

The player with the lowest total score after all the games have been played is the winner.

Stretch

What's unique: At the end of each hand, all players count the total number of pips on the tiles, if any, remaining in their hand. That number is then subtracted from their own score, unlike in most games where that number would be added to the winner's score.

Playing with this variation does lengthen the game. Hence, the appropriate name—Stretch.

Use the rules to Block, Draw, Muggins, or many other games, with this exception:

At the end of each hand, players count the total

number of pips on the tiles, if any, remaining in their hand and that number is then subtracted from their own score.

Latin American Match Dominoes

What's unique: Each hand that is won counts as one game, and a match ends when a team has won at least 10 games.

Domino set: Double-6.

Play this game using the rules to Block with these variations:

Number of players: 4 players play as 2 teams of 2 players per team.

Set: Player holding the 6-6 makes the first play with that tile.

Although each hand that is won counts as one game, and a match ends when one team has won at least 10 games, a match win is scored only if the other team failed to win 5 games. In which case, the match is considered to end with a tie.

Cuban Dominoes

Block game with these exceptions:

Domino set: Played with double-9.

Number of dominoes drawn: 4 players draw 10 tiles each. The remaining 15 tiles stay in the boneyard and are not drawn.

Set: Highest double starts play. After the set, play continues to the right (counterclockwise).

Doubles

What's unique: Before playing any tile from your hand, there must already be a double in the layout of the same suit as the matching end of the tile you wish to play.

This game is played using the rules to Draw with the following exceptions:

Set: The player who is holding the heaviest double leads with that tile. The set double is a spinner. Before you can play any tile from your hand, there must already be a double in the layout of the same suit as the matching end of the tile that you wish to play.

Here is an example, a player wishes to play the 3-4 tile in his or her hand by matching the 3 end to another tile in the layout with an exposed end of 3. A player can only do this if the 3-3 has already been played and is, therefore, in the layout. There does not have to be a 4-4 in the layout because the other end of the 3-4 tile the player wishes to play (the 4 end) is not the end of the tile that is being matched in that particular play.

Tiddle-a-Wink

(aka Tiddly-Wink)

What's unique: After you play a double, you have the option to play another tile (the Block game with this one exception).

Number of players: 2 or more.

Excellent party game for 3 to 6 individual players. May also be played by teams.

Domino Pool

What's unique: The game is played with a pool.

This is the Block game with these exceptions:

Number of players: 2 or more. Ex-cellent party game for 3 to 6 individual players. May also be played by teams.

Number of dominoes drawn: Divide the tiles between the players, leaving at least 8 dominoes in the bone-yard. For example: If 3 players, draw 6 tiles; 4 players, draw 5; 5 players, draw 4; 6 players, draw 3.

Set: Draw lots to determine who makes the first play. Any domino can be set.Before the game begins, each player puts an equal, agreed-upon, amount of money (or number of chips, dried beans, etc.) into the pool. And, once the pool has been won, each player puts an equal, agreed-upon, amount of money into the pool again before beginning the next game.

Scoring: The winner of the hand gets the pool. The winner of the hand is 1) the first player to domino;

or (2) the player with the smallest count left in his hand, if the game ends in a block. In the event the low count is tied in a game ending in a block, the pool is divided among the low hands.

Variation: The first player or team to reach 100 points wins the pool.

Matador

(aka Master Dominoes, Seven-Up, Russian Cross, Russian Dominoes, and All Sevens.

What's unique: The sum of the tiles touching sides in the layout must total 7. (This is the Block game with this one exception.)

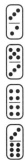

Blind Dominoes

(aka Blind Hughie, Secret Dominoes, Blind-Man Block, and Billiton)

It's obvious why the game goes by the names of Blind or Secret Dominoes: Players don't know what tiles they hold in their hand and are unable to choose their play. But what about the name Billiton? The word is the anglicized spelling of Belitung, an island off the former Dutch colony of Sumatra, so maybe this game was a pastime of the Dutch colonists or was an Oriental import.

What's unique: A player doesn't see his hand until he plays it.

Number of players: 2 to 4 players.

Number of dominoes drawn: 2 players, draw 14; 3 players, draw 9; 4 players, draw 7. The entire deck is drawn, except with 3 players, when the one undrawn tile is set.

Variation: 2 players, draw 8; 3 players, draw 7; 4 players, draw 6. Remaining tiles are discarded.

Set: Draw lots to determine who makes the first play.

How to play: Each player draws his tiles from the boneyard without looking at the face of the domino. Keeping the tiles facedown on the table, each player arranges his tiles (1) in a vertical row, long side to long side, playing his tiles one at a time from the top of his row or from the bottom of his row; or (2) in a horizontal row, long side to long side, playing tiles from his row in any order he chooses. Players should decide at the beginning of the game whether they want to play from top to bottom, bottom to top, or in any order the players choose.

Let's say the players have decided to play from top to bottom, and Mark is the first player. Mark turns over his first tile, the tile on the top of his vertical row. Then he turns over a second tile, the next tile in his row. If he is able to play his second tile on his first tile by matching suits, he does so. He continues to turn over tiles as long as he is able to make a play. And, if he turns over a tile that can be played on more than one end of the line of play, he may turn over and look at the next tile in his row before choosing where to play his domino. If he turns over a tile that he is unable to play, he places it facedown at the bottom of his row. If the tile Mark turned over and was unable to play happens to be a double, he places it faceup at the bottom of his row. Then, play continues with the next player, the one at Mark's left.

Variations: (1). During his turn, a player may choose to play any exposed double in his row. (2.) A player's turn does not continue as long as he can make a play. Instead, a player is only allowed to turn over one tile per turn. (3.) If playing the variation of turning over any tile of your choosing from your row (as opposed to playing from top to bottom or from bottom to top), when an unplayable tile is exposed during your turn, that tile is turned facedown and placed on the left end of your horizontal row.

Other rules:

- There are no spinners. (Variation: Only the first double played is a spinner.)
- Game ends when one player dominoes or when the game is blocked.

Tip: If playing the variation of turning over any tile of your choosing from your row (as opposed to play-ing from top to bottom or from bottom to top), it is certainly a help to the player's game if he can remember the position of the previously exposed tiles and therefore be able to turn them over during his turn when there is an open end in the line of play with a matching suit to the tile in his hand.

SAME, BUT DIFFERENT

Cross Dominoes, Sebastopol, Cyprus, The Fortress, and *Maltese Cross* are all very similar games. In each of these games, a cross or star shape must be formed by playing tiles off the set domino before any other tiles may be played in any other direction.*

In some places, a game that goes by the name of "The Fortress" or simply "Fortress" uses the iden-tical rules as the game of Sebastopol. In other places, "The Fortress" uses the identical rules as the game of Cyprus, which, in that particular case, is nicknamed "Sebastopol with Double-9's." Although their versions of Sebastopol and

Cyprus are very much alike, I don't feel that they are similar enough to say that Cyprus is Sebastopol with Double-9's. Their version of the game of Sebastopol creates a 5-tile cross with the double-6 as the set domino in the first rounds of the game, and their game of Fortress creates a 9-tile cross with the double-9 as the set domino in the first rounds of the game.

Merry-Go-Round is a variation of Cross Dominoes and Five-Up. You'll find the rules to Merry-Go-Round and Five-Up in the section in this chapter on Scoring Games.

Cross Dominoes

(aka Cross)

What's unique: The first double played is a spinner and it must be played on both ends and both sides, forming a 5-tile cross, before any other tile can be played.

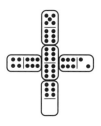

Variation: If after the first round of play not all four sides of the first double have been played upon, in subsequent rounds no tile can be played on the remaining open end (or ends) of the first double played.

Number of dominoes drawn: 2 players, draw 7; 3 players, draw 6; 4 players, draw 5.

Variation: Each player draws 6 tiles and the remaining tiles are discarded. In this game variation, if you cannot make a play, you must pass.

Set: The player holding the highest double makes the first play.

Other rules:

- Only the first double played is a spinner.
- A player may not pass if he is holding a playable tile in his hand.
- If a player cannot make a play, he must draw from the boneyard until he draws a playable domino. Do not draw the last two remaining dominoes in the boneyard.
- If a player cannot make a play, he must pass if (1) he was unable to draw a playable domino; (2) there are only two dominoes left in the boneyard, and therefore no more dominoes left to be

drawn; or (3) playing the variation mentioned above, in which all players draw 6 tiles each and then must pass if a play cannot be made.

- Game ends when a player dominoes or when game is blocked.

Variation: The player who makes the first play by setting the highest double has the option to immediately add another tile to the set tile or to pass.

Cyprus

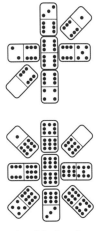

What's unique: The highest double is played as set. The set domino must be played on both ends, both sides, and diagonally, forming a 7-tile star with a double-6 set of dominoes or a 9-tile star with a double-9 or double-12 set, before any other tile can be played. This is the Block game with the above and the set exception.

Set: The player holding the highest double begins.

Maltese Cross

(aka Double Cross)

What's unique: The highest double is played as set. The set domino must be played on both ends and both sides, forming a 5-tile cross, before any other tile can be played. Next, a double must be played on each of the four tiles that are played from the set double before play continues with the rules to Block.

This is the Block game with the above and the set exception.

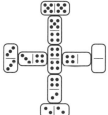

Set: The player holding the highest double begins play.

Sebastopol

(aka Malakoff)

What's unique: The 6-6 is played as set. The 6-6 is a spinner and must be played on both ends and both sides, forming a 5-tile cross, before any other tile can be played.

This is the Block game with the above and the set exception.

Set: The player who is holding the 6-6 domino begins play.

The Fortress

What's unique: This game is played with a double-9 set of dominoes; the double-9 is set domino; and 8 dominoes from the 9 suit must be played on the double-9 domino before any other tiles can be played.

Number of players: Best with 6 players; may be played with 4.

Number of dominoes drawn: 6 players, draw 9; 4 players, draw 13. If 6 are playing, the player to set the double-9 gets the remaining tile in the bone-yard and plays again before the second player makes his play. If 4 are playing, the player to set the double-9 gets 1 of the 3 remaining tiles in the boneyard and plays again before the second player makes his play.

Object of the game: 6 players, draw 7; 4 players, draw 9.

Set: Double-9.

Other rules: If the double-9 tile is in the boneyard because it was not drawn when players drew their hands, let the player who lost the last hand draw from the boneyard and then set the double-9 tile.

No spinners except the set domino, double-9, which is played on 8 sides.

Game score can be 100, 150, or 200 points.

Chickenfoot®

(© 1987 by Louis and Betty Howsley)

Domino set: Double-9 set.

Number of players: 2 and up.

This is the game of Draw with these exceptions:

What's unique: Two different formations are made: the double chickenfoot and the chickenfoot. The double chickenfoot is made at the beginning of each hand by playing 6 tiles diagonally, 3 on each side, of the set tile. Chickenfoots are made throughout the hand by playing 3 tiles diagonally on one side of a double played during the game. Tiles played diagonally on the double tile are called "chicken-toes." A chickenfoot or a double chickenfoot must have all the chickentoes before any other plays can be made.

Also unique: 50 points are added to your score at the end of a hand if you are left holding the 0-0 tile.

Object of the game: To be the player with the lowest score at the end of the game.

Number of tiles drawn: Each player draws an equal number of tiles from the "chicken yard." For example: If 2 play, each draws 20 tiles; if 8 play, each draws 6 tiles. There are 55 tiles in the set. Tiles left after each player draws remain in the chicken yard to be drawn from during the hand.

Set: Player holding the 9-9 makes the first play of the game. Subsequent games would begin with the next-lowest double tile (8-8; 7-7; 6-6; and so on, the last game beginning with the 0-0 tile). If no one holds the correct double tile to begin that particular hand, players may agree to either (1) go to the next-lowest double (for example, 8-8 in the case of the first play of the game) or (2) reshuffle all the tiles and draw new hands. Play continues to the left.

The next 6 plays must be made on the 9-9 tile, 3 tiles played diagonally on each side of the 9-9 tile. This formation is called a "double chickenfoot." To do this, players must match a tile from their hand of the 9 suit to the 9-9 set tile.

If 6 tiles have not been played on the 9-9 set and a player does not hold a tile from the 9 suit in his hand, he may draw one tile from the chicken yard. If he draws a tile with a 9 end, he plays it on the set tile. If he does not draw a tile from the 9 suit, he must pass his turn to the player on his left.

After 6 tiles have been played on the 9-9 set tile, plays can be made on any of the 6 chickentoes by matching tiles end to end, until someone plays a double tile.

Once a double tile has been played on one of the chickentoes, the next three plays must be made on the double tile before plays can be made anywhere else in the layout. This formation of 3 tiles played

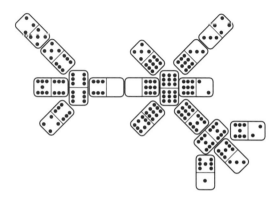

on the double tile is called a chickenfoot.

Once the new chickenfoot has been completed by playing 3 tiles diagonally on one side of a double tile, players may return to adding tiles to any of the chickentoes until someone plays another double.

The game ends once a player plays all the tiles in his hand or when the game ends in block because none of the players are able to make a play and there are no tiles in the chicken yard to draw from. Players must count the dots on the tiles remaining in their hand (1 point per 1 dot) and record their score. Remember, the player caught having the 0-0 gets 50 points.

For the next hand, tiles are reshuffled and each player draws the same number of tiles from the chicken yard as he or she did at the beginning of the previous hand played. The second hand begins with the 8-8 tile; the third hand, with the 7-7 tile; and so on.

For a longer game, players may choose to continue playing by starting another hand with the 1-1 tile following the hand that began with the 0-0 tile as set. Subsequent hands would begin with the next-highest double played as set (2-2; 3-3; and so on, up to the last hand beginning with the 9-9 tile).

Fours

What's unique: This game is for four players only and each must play individually and not as a team. Also, players can continue to play as long as they can make a match.

How to play: Play by the rules to Block with these exceptions.

Number of players: 4 players, each playing individually, no teams. The first player is determined by lot. Anytime a player makes a play, he may continue to play as long as he can make a match.

Add-'Em-Up 50

What's unique: When a player plays a tile that matches an open end in the line of play, the number of pips on the tile's open end is added to his score, and the first player to reach 50 or more points is the winner and yells, "Domino!"

Number of dominoes drawn: Each player draws 5 tiles.

Set: Any tile may be set and is set by the last person to draw from the boneyard.

If the first player sets a double, he earns points of the total number of pips on that tile; if it is a single, he earns points of the total number of pips on the heaviest end of the tile. Play then continues to his left.

The next player makes a play by matching one of the ends of the set tile with one of the ends of a tile from his hand. This player earns points of the total number of pips on the exposed end of his tile (the end that does not match the set tile). Play continues, clockwise around the table, in this manner.

Any time a player is unable to make a play, he must draw from the boneyard until he draws a playable tile. A player must pass if there are no tiles left in the boneyard and he holds no playable tile in his hand.

The first player to reach 50 or more points is the winner and gets to shout, "Domino!"

Variations: You may change the number of points a player must receive in order to win the game. To shorten or lengthen the game, make the number of points to win lower or higher than 50 points. In the case of a longer game: If all tiles in the deck have been played before any player reaches the winning score, start a new game, but add points earned to your score from the previous game(s).

Pass

What's unique: A player has the option of passing up his turn and not making a play even when he holds a playable tile in his hand and/or there are still available tiles in the boneyard. (Play by the rules for Draw with this one exception.)

One-Arm Joe

What's unique: Plays can only be made on one side of the set tile.

Number of players: Any number, however 5 to 9 players is best. Those playing may chose to play in teams of two, three, or four per team.

Object of the game: To be the first to domino.

Number of dominoes drawn: Each player draws 3 tiles.

Set: Player with highest double.

Any time a player makes a play on a double, including the set double, he may play a second tile before his turn is up.

When a player cannot make a play, he or she

should draw from the boneyard until drawing a playable tile. If there are no tiles left in the boneyard to draw from and the player has no playable tile in his hand, he must pass.

The first player to play all tiles in his hand announces, "Domino!"

If a game ends in a block, all the players turn their dominoes faceup, count the pips on each tile, and add the numbers together. The player who dominoed, or the player with the lowest total if the game ended in a block, wins the game and gets the points of all the other players.

The player who gets 100 points or more first is the overall winner.

SCORING GAMES

All the games in this section are called scoring games because scoring is done during play and at the end of each hand.

In these several games, a player is awarded points every time he makes a play that results in the open ends of the tiles in the line of play adding up to a multiple of 5: Muggins, All Fives, Five-Up, Sniff, Seven-Toed Pete, and Merry-Go-Round.

In the game of All Threes, points are awarded to a player when he makes a play that results in the open ends of the tiles in the line of play adding up to a multiple of 3; and, in the game of Threes and Fives, points are awarded for multiples of 3 and multiples of 5.

In the game of Bergen, points are scored by a player after he makes a play resulting in both open ends of the tiles in the line of play being alike.

All the games in this section, with the exception of Bergen, are very similar. And, just like most of the domino games in this book, sometimes the identical game rules go by two or more different names depending on what country or what part of a country you are in. Sometimes games that go by the same name aren't played with the same rules. Then there are also many, many different variations of certain games that go by a slightly different, but very similar, name.

Here are some examples of what I found in my research.

Five different domino game instruction books state that what makes the game of All Fives unique from all other games in the "five-point family" of games is that when hands are drawn at the beginning of the game, only five tiles per player are drawn regardless of the number of players. Yet, in another book written by a group of authors most consider to be experts, players of the game of All Fives are instructed to draw 7 tiles each if there are 2 playing and 5 tiles each if there are 3 or 4 players.

The very thing that is said to make the game of Five-Up unique from all other games in the "five-point family" of games is that every double played is a spinner. Yet I found rules to the game in one place that make no mention at all that every double played is a spinner.

I could give many more such examples. For this book, I have attempted to list variations of rules. When I found rules that contradict each other, as in the examples above, I went with the most-often-noted rules.

Unless otherwise indicated, the games here use the following rules:

- One set of double-6 dominoes (28 pieces) is used.
- Shuffle the dominoes, facedown, at the beginning of each hand.
- Object of the game: To gain the highest score possible by making points while playing the game and by being the first player to domino.

Muggins

What's unique: If a player should overlook a score, his opponent may call "Muggins!" and take the score himself.

Number of players: 2 to 4 players. The game may be played in partnership when there are 4 players.

Number of dominoes drawn: If 2 play, each player draws 7 tiles. If 3 or 4 play, each player draws 5 tiles.

Variations: (1) No more than 4 can play, and every player, regardless of the number of players, draws 7 tiles. (2) If 4 play, each draws 5 tiles; if 3 play, each draws 6; and, if 2 play, each draws 7.

The tiles not drawn are pushed to one side to make up the boneyard.

Set: Lots are drawn to determine who sets the first tile. The first player may play any domino in his hand. After the first tile has been set, play continues to the left.

Variation: The player holding the highest double in his hand makes the first play by setting that tile. After the first tile has been set, play continues to the left.

The first double played is a spinner.

Variation: There are no spinners.

How to Play: After the first domino is set, subsequent players must join a tile from their hand with an open end in the line of play. The ends of the two tiles that are joined must have the same number of pips.

If a player is unable to make a play from his hand, he must draw tiles from the boneyard until he draws a playable tile. If a player is unable to make a play from his hand and there are no tiles left in the boneyard, the player must skip his turn until he is able to make a play.

Variations: (1) When there are 2 players, the last two tiles in the boneyard may not be drawn. If there are 3 or 4 players, the last tile in the boneyard may not be drawn. (2) If a player has a playable tile, he must play it. (3) A player may draw from the boneyard even if he holds a playable tile in his hand.

Scoring: A player is awarded points every time he makes a play that results in the open ends of the tiles in the line of play adding up to a multiple of 5. (5 points for 5 pips; 10 points for 10 pips; 15 points for 15 pips; and so on.) Each player must announce his points on making his play in order to receive credit for the points made. If a player overlooks a score, his opponent may call, "Muggins!" and take the score himself.

The player who dominoes is also awarded points at the end of each hand by adding up, and rounding to the nearest multiple of 5, the pips on the tiles left in his opponents' hands: 1 or 2 pips is worth nothing; 3, 4, 5, 6, and 7 is worth 5 points; 8, 9, 10, 11, and 12 is worth 10 points; and so on. The first player, or partnership if 4 are playing, to reach 200 points wins the game. If a player reaches 200 points during play, the game ends at that point. If points are tallied at the end of a hand and more than one player has a score of 200 or more, the player with the highest score wins. In case of a tie, follow these rules: If 2 are playing, play two more hands; 3 players, play three more hands; 4 players, play four more hands.

Variations: (1) The first to reach 100 points wins the game. (2) A player is awarded one point every time he makes a play that results in the open ends of the tiles in the line of play adding up to a multiple of 5. (1 point for 5 pips; 2 points for 10 pips; 3 points for 15 pips; and so on.) The player who dominoes is also awarded points—one point for each multiple of 5—at the end of each hand by adding up, and rounding to the nearest multiple of 5, the pips on the tiles left in his opponents' hands. The first player, or partnership if 4 are playing, to reach exactly 61 points wins the game. If any play made causes the player's or partnership's total score to exceed 61 points, then no points at all are scored for that particular play, and play continues to the left. (3) If a larger group is playing, players may wish to reduce the number of points that must be reached in order to win the game. The number of points to be reached must be agreed upon by all the players prior to the start of the game.

Scoring if hand is blocked: Each player counts the pips on the remaining tiles in his hand. The player with the lowest number of pips scores the difference between his total and that of each of his opponents.

Then, the player with the next-lowest number of pips scores the difference between his total and that of each of his opponents, and so on.

Variations: (1) The player with the lowest number of pips scores the total number of pips in his opponent's hand. If there is a tie for the lowest number of pips, there is no score. (2) The player with the lowest number of pips wins the game.

Scoring when partners play: Players must play individually, but a common score is kept for partners. When one player dominoes, the number of pips on the tiles remaining in the hand of his partner are subtracted from their score.

All Fives

What's unique: Players draw 5 tiles from the stock regardless of the number of players.

Number of players: 2 to 4 players. The game may be played in partnership when there are 4 players.

Number of dominoes drawn: Players draw 5 tiles from the stock regardless of the number of players.

The tiles not drawn are pushed to one side to make up the boneyard.

Set: Lots are drawn to determine who sets the first tile. The first player may play any domino in his hand. After the first tile has been set, play continues to the left.

The first double played is a spinner.

How to play: After the first domino is set, subsequent players must join a tile from their hand with an open end in the line of play. The ends of the two tiles that are joined must have the same number of pips.

If a player is unable to make a play from his hand, he must draw tiles from the boneyard until he draws a playable tile. If a player is unable to make a play from his hand and there are no tiles left in the boneyard, the player must skip his turn until he is able to make a play.

Variations: (1) When there are 2 players, the last two tiles in the boneyard may not be drawn. If there are 3 or 4 players, the last tile in the boneyard may not be drawn. (2) If a player has a playable tile, he must play it. (3) If a player plays a tile that scores points or if a player plays a double, he plays another tile from his hand before the next player takes a turn. If he is unable to play another tile from his hand, he draws from the boneyard until he draws a playable tile or until the boneyard is exhausted. (4) A player cannot "domino" with a scoring tile or a double. If he plays the last tile in his hand and it is a double or a scoring tile, he must draw from the boneyard until he draws a playable tile or until the boneyard is exhausted. If the boneyard is already exhausted at the time the player would play his last piece, he must skip his turn, and play continues to the left.

Scoring: A player is awarded points every time he makes a play that results in the open ends of the tiles in the line of play adding up to a multiple of 5. (5 points for 5 pips; 10 points for 10 pips; 15 points for 15 pips; and so on.) The player who dominoes is also awarded points at the end of each hand by adding up, and rounding to the nearest multiple of 5, the pips on the tiles left in his opponents' hands. Only 1 or 2 pips is worth nothing; 3, 4, 5, 6, and 7 is worth 5 points; 8, 9, 10, 11, and 12 is worth 10 points; and so on. The first player, or partnership if 4 are playing, to reach 200 points wins the game. If a player reaches 200 points during play, the game ends at that point. If points are tallied at the end of a hand and more than one player has a score of 200 or more, the player with the highest score wins. In case of a tie, follow these rules: If 2 are playing, play two more hands; 3 players, play three more hands; 4 players, play four more hands.

Variations: (1) The first to reach 150 points wins the game. (2) First to reach 250 points wins the game. (3) A player is awarded one point every time he makes a play that results in the open ends of the tiles in the line of play adding up to a multiple of 5. (1 point for 5 pips; 2 points for 10 pips; 3 points for 15 pips; and so on.) The player who dominoes is also awarded points—one point for each multiple of 5—at the end of each hand by adding up, and rounding to the nearest multiple of 5, the pips on the tiles left in his opponents' hands. The first player, or partnership if 4 are playing, to reach exactly 61 points wins the game. If any play made causes the player's or partnership's total score to exceed 61 points, then no points at all are scored for that particular play and play continues to the left. (4) If a larger group is playing, players may wish to reduce the number of points that must be reached in order to win the game. The reduced number of points needed must be agreed upon by all the players prior to the start of the game. 5) The number of pips on the open end of a just-played tile may be subtracted from the total of the other ends of the layout, instead of being added, to make a multiple of five.

Scoring if hand is blocked: Each player counts the pips on the remaining tiles in his hand. The player with the lowest number of pips scores the difference between his total and that of each of his opponents. Then, the player with the next-lowest number of pips scores the difference between his total and that of each of his opponents, and so on.

Variations: The player with the lowest number of

pips scores the total number of pips in his oppo nents' hands. If there is a tie for the lowest number of pips in a two-handed or four-handed game, there is no score. If there is a tie for the lowest number of pips in a three-handed game, the number of pips in their opponent's hand is split evenly between them.

Scoring when partners play: Players must play individually, but a common score is kept for partners. When a player dominoes, the number of pips on the tiles remaining in the hand of his partner are subtracted from their score.

Five-Up

(aka West Coast Dominoes in U.S.)

This game was created over fifty years ago in the San Francisco area, which has, since 1969, been headquarters to the International Domino Association (IDA). The game's popularity can be attributed to Dominic Armanino, the author of several domino game instruction books, including one devoted entirely to the game of Five-Up. Mr. Armanino was also a founder of the IDA, and Five-Up has always been the game played at IDA-sponsored tournaments.

What's unique: Every double played is a possible spinner.

Number of players: 2 to 4 players. The game may be played in partnership when there are 4 players.

Number of dominoes drawn: 5. *Variation:* If 2 play, each player draws 7 tiles. If 3 or 4 play, each player draws 5 tiles.

The tiles not drawn are pushed to one side to make up the boneyard.

Set: Lots are drawn to determine who sets the first tile. The first player may play any domino in his hand. After the first tile has been set, play continues to the left.

Every double played is a possible spinner.

How to play: After the first domino is set, subsequent players must join a tile from their hand with an open end in the line of play. The ends of the two tiles that are joined must have the same number of pips.

If a player is unable to make a play from his hand, he must draw tiles from the boneyard until he draws a playable tile. If a

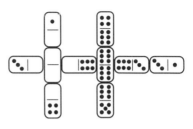

player is unable to make a play from his hand and there are no tiles left in the boneyard, the player must skip his turn until he is able to make a play. *Variations:* (1) When there are 2 players, the last two tiles in the boneyard may not be drawn. If there are 3 or 4 players, the last tile in the boneyard may not be drawn. (2) If a player has a playable tile, he must play it.

Scoring: A player is awarded one point every time he makes a play that results in the open ends of the tiles in the line of play adding up to a multiple of 5. (1 point for 5 pips; 2 points for 10 pips; 3 points for 15 pips; and so on.) The player who dominoes is also awarded points—one point for each multiple of 5—at the end of each hand by adding up, and rounding to the nearest multiple of 5, the pips on the tiles left in his opponents' hands: 1 or 2 pips is worth nothing; 3, 4, 5, 6, and 7 is worth 1 point; 8, 9, 10, 11, and 12 is worth 2 points, and so on. The first player, or partnership if 4 are playing, to reach exactly 61 points wins the game. If any play made causes the player's or partnership's total score to exceed 61 points, then no points at all are scored for that particular play, and play continues to the left.

Variation: If a larger group is playing, players may wish to reduce the number of points that must be reached in order to win the game. The number of points to be reached must be agreed upon by all the players prior to the start of the game.

Scoring if hand is blocked: Each player counts the pips on the remaining tiles in his or her hand. The player with the lowest number of pips scores the difference between his total and that of each of his opponents. Then the player with the next-lowest number of pips scores the difference between his total and that of each of his opponents, and so on.

Variations: The player with the lowest number of pips scores the total number of pips in his opponent's hand. If there is a tie for the lowest number of pips in a two-handed or four-handed game, there is no score. If there is a tie for the lowest number of pips in a three-handed game, the number of pips in their opponent's hand is split evenly between them.

Scoring when partners play: Players must play individually, but a common score is kept for partners. When one player dominoes, the number of pips on the tiles remaining in the hand of his partner are subtracted from their score.

Sniff

(aka as East Coast Dominoes in U.S. and Partnership Dominoes)

What's unique: The first, and only the first, domino played is a spinner, or "sniff." The pips on any open end of the sniff are counted for points until plays have been made on all four ends.

Number of players: 2 to 4 players; the game may be played in partnership when there are 4 players.

Number of dominoes drawn: If 2 play, each player draws 7 tiles. If 3 or 4 play, each player draws 5 tiles.

Variations: (1) No more than 4 can play and every player draws 7 tiles. (2) If 4 play, each draws 5 tiles; if 3 play, each draws 6; and, if 2 play, each draws 7.

The tiles not drawn are pushed to one side to make up the boneyard.

Set: Lots are drawn to determine who sets the first tile. The first player may play any domino in his hand. After the first tile has been set, play continues to the left.

Variation: The player holding the highest double in his hand makes the first play by setting that tile. After the first tile has been set, play continues to the left.

The first double played is a spinner.

Scoring: A player is awarded points every time he makes a play that results in the open ends of the tiles in the line of play adding up to a multiple of 5. (5 points for 5 pips; 10 points for 10 pips; 15 points for 15 pips; and so on.) The player who dominoes is also awarded points at the end of each hand by adding up, and rounding to the nearest multiple of 5, the pips on the tiles left in his opponents' hands. 1 or 2 pips is worth nothing; 3, 4, 5, 6, and 7 is worth 1 point; 8, 9, 10, 11, and 12 is worth 2 points, and so on. The first player, or partnership if 4 are playing, to reach 200 points wins the game.

Variations: (1) First to reach 100 points wins the game. (2) A player is awarded one point every time he makes a play that results in the open ends of the tiles in the line of play adding up to a multiple of 5. (1 point for 5 pips; 2 points for 10 pips; 3 points for 15 pips; and so on.) The player who dominoes is also awarded points—one point for each multiple of 5—at the end of each hand by adding up, and rounding to the nearest multiple of 5, the pips on the tiles left in his opponents' hands. The first player, or partnership if 4 are playing, to reach exactly 61 points wins the game. If any play made causes the player's or partnership's total score to exceed 61 points, then no points at all are scored for that particular play and play continues to the left. (3) If a larger group is playing, players may wish to reduce the number of points that must be reached in order to win the game. The number of points to be reached must be agreed upon by all the players prior to the start of the game.

All Threes

What's unique: A player is awarded points every time he makes a play that results in the open ends of the tiles in the line of play adding up to a multiple of 3.

Number of players: 2 to 4 players. 4 players may play as two teams of 2 players per team.

The tiles not drawn are pushed to one side to make up the boneyard.

Set: Lots are drawn to determine who sets the first tile. The first player may play any domino in his hand. After the first tile has been set, play continues to the left.

The first double played is a spinner.

Scoring: A player is awarded points every time he makes a play that results in the open ends of the tiles in the line of play adding up to a multiple of 3. (3 points for 3 pips; 6 points for 6 pips; 9 points for 9 pips; and so on.) The player who dominoes is also awarded points at the end of each hand by adding up, and rounding to the nearest multiple of 3, the pips on the tiles left in his opponents' hands. 1 pip is worth nothing; 2, 3, and 4 is worth 3 points; 5, 6, and 7 is worth 6 points; and so on. The first player, or partnership if 4 are playing, to reach 200 points wins the game.

Variations: (1) The first player to reach 150 points wins the game. (2) First to reach 250 points wins the game. (3) A player is awarded one point every time he makes a play that results in the open ends of the tiles in the line of play adding up to a multiple of 3. (1 point for 3 pips; 2 points for 6 pips; 3 points for 9 pips; and so on.) The player who dominoes is also awarded points—one point for each multiple of 3—at the end of each hand by adding up, and rounding to the nearest multiple of 3, the pips on the tiles left in his opponents' hands. The first player, or partnership if 4 are playing, to reach exactly 61 points wins the game. If any play made causes the player's or partnership's total score to exceed 61 points, then no points at all are scored for that particular play, and play continues to the left. (4) If a larger group is playing, players may wish to reduce the number of points that must be reached in order to win the game. The number of points to be reached must be agreed upon by all the players prior to the start of the game.

Seven-Toed Pete

(aka Racehorse and Seven Go)

What's unique: If a player plays a double or one of the 5 scoring dominoes (6-4, 5-5, 5-0, 4-1, or 3-2), he may continue to play tiles from his hand.

Object of the game: To make the total count of the exposed ends of tiles played equal 5 or a multiple of 5.

This is the same game as Five-Up, but with three variations.

Number of players: 2 to 4 players. 4 players may play as two teams of 2 players per team.

Number of dominoes drawn: 7 tiles per player.

Set: First player must play a double tile or a score tile. If the first player is unable to play a double tile or a score tile to set, he (1) passes if there are 4 players, or (2) draws from the boneyard if there are 2 or 3 players.

Scoring: 1 point for every multiple of 5. For example: A total of 5 pips on the exposed ends of the tiles in the layout is worth 1 point; 10 pips is worth 2 points; 15 pips, 3 points.

When a player plays a double or a score tile, including the set domino, he must play again.

A player may play any matching tile in his hand to the set domino. If he scores or plays a double, he must make another play or (1) pass if there are 4 players, or (2) draw from the boneyard until he draws a playable tile if there are 2 or 3 players.

In a game of 2 or 3 players, if a player's last tile is a double or a score tile, he must play it and then draw from the boneyard until he draws another playable tile. In the case of a two-handed game, he must leave 2 tiles in the boneyard; in a three-handed game, 1 tile. If he does not hold a playable tile and there are no more available tiles in the boneyard, he must pass. Play continues until one player has played the last tile in his hand, and it is not a double tile or a score tile.

In a game of 4 players, if a player's last tile is a double or a score tile, he is "washed up." The other players continue to play until one player has played the last tile in his hand, and it is not a double tile or a score tile.

The game is over when one player dominoes or when the game is blocked. The player or team with the lowest number of pips left in his hand (0 in the case of a player who has dominoed) is the winner and receives 1 point for every pip left on the remaining tiles in his opponents' hands.

Threes and Fives

What's unique: A player is awarded points every time he makes a play that results in the open ends of the tiles in the line of play adding up to a multiple of 3 or a multiple of 5.

Play by the rules of Muggins, with these exceptions.

A player scores 1 point per pip when the total number of pips on the exposed ends of the tiles in the layout is a multiple of 3 or a multiple of 5. If, after making a play, the

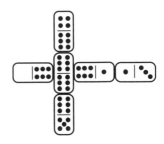

total number of pips on the exposed ends of tiles in the layout total 10, which is a multiple of 5, that player would score 10 points. If the total number of pips was 12, which is a multiple of 3, that player would score 12 points. If the total number of pips was 30, a multiple of 3 and a multiple of 5, that player would score 60 points (30+30).

The game is over when one player has dominoed or when the game is blocked. Once the game is over, each player should count the total number of pips on the remaining tiles in his hand. The player who dominoed or the player left with the lowest number of pips in his hand at the end of the game is the winner. The winner earns a score of the total number of pips left in his opponents' hands (1 point per 1 pip).

The game is usually 251 points.

Merry-Go-Round

What's unique: A double must be set and the succeeding plays must be made on both sides, first, and then on both ends of the set tile, until all four sides have been played on.

Number of players: 2 to 4 players.

Number of dominoes drawn: Each player draws 7 tiles.

Set: The first player must set a double. If he does not hold a double in his hand, he must draw from the boneyard until he draws a double and then use that double to make his first play.

After a tile has been played on each of the four sides of the set domino, plays may be made on any exposed end, in any order, with a single or a double tile.

Play by the rules to Five-Up with the above exceptions.

Bergen

(aka Double-Header)

Bergen is German for mountains. Because the game is sometimes referred to as "the Bergen game," there is reason to believe it did not originate in Germany, but might have come instead from

Bergen op Zoom, a coastal town in the Netherlands, or from Bergen, Norway.

What's unique: Both open ends of the layout must be made alike.

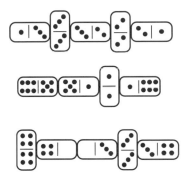

Number of players: 2 to 4.

Same as for the Block game or Muggins, with the following exceptions:

Number of dominoes drawn: Each player draws 6 tiles.

You *must* make both open ends of the layout alike.

TRUMP AND TRICK GAMES

The games in this section are very different from those games categorized as "blocking" and "scoring" games. Tiles are not matched on the table to form a layout. Instead, they are ranked by suit; trumps are named; tricks are taken; and in all but one game in this section, players bid on their hand.

The most popular of all the what I call "trump and trick" games is the game of Forty-Two. Numerous bidding variations for the game of Forty-Two have been created—to name a few: Big Bertha; Cajun Hokey Pokey; Eagle Eye; East Lansing Deferred-Style Nillo; Follow Me; Inverted Low Boy; Low; Low Boy; Multiple Trumps Forty-Two; Naperville Onesies; Near-Seven; No Catchem; No Trump; Splash; and West Texas Rules. In this section, I will give a brief description of three bidding variations: Sevens, Plunge, and Nel-O (sometimes spelled Nillo).

Unless otherwise indicated: one set of double-6 dominoes (28 pieces) is used.

The dominoes are shuffled, facedown, at the beginning of each hand.

Forty-Two

(aka Texas Forty-Two, Four-Hand Texas, and Domino Rounce)

Forty-Two is an adaptation of Auction Pitch. It was invented by W. A. Thomas during his boyhood in Garner, Parker County, Texas, about 1885; then it spread throughout the southwestern United States.

In this game, if a team collects each of the 7 tricks (1 point per trick) and each of the 5-count dominoes (2 tiles worth 10 points each and 3 tiles worth 5 points each, for a total of 35 points) in the course of one hand, he will have a total of 42 points (7 + 35 = 42). Thus, the name of the game.

Object of the game: To be the first team to reach 250 points.

Number of players: 4 players play as 2 teams of 2 players per team.

Draw lots at the beginning of the game to determine which player shuffles first. Reshuffle the tiles. *Number of dominoes drawn:* Each player draws 7 tiles. All players, except for the shuffler, simultaneously draw 7 tiles from the deck. The shuffler, then, draws the 7 remaining tiles.

The person to the shuffler's left has the first option to bid.

Your bid is a prediction of how many of the 42 points you will win in that hand. Your bid should be based almost entirely on your own hand. However, if you win the bid, any points won by your partner during that hand will also count towards your bid.

If you hold at least 3 tiles from the same suit in your hand, that is considered a potential bidding hand. That suit will be your trump suit if you win the bid. If you hold 1 or 2 doubles as well as 3 tiles from the same suit, this is considered a strong hand.

The word "trump" comes from the word "triumph." A domino from the trump suit automatically "triumphs" over other dominoes played.

Once trumps for the hand have been declared, all 7 dominoes of that suit rank higher than all 21 other dominoes. Regardless of who plays it, the highest trump played wins any trick. A trump domino only belongs to the trump suit and not also to the other suit represented on its face. The other number on the trump domino only serves to rank trumps among themselves.

For example: If fours are trumps, the 4-4 is the strongest domino of the hand; the 4-6 beats the 4-5; the 4-5 beats the 4-3; and so on, the 4-0 being the lowest trump. The 4-0 for that hand would beat any tile that is not from the 4 suit.

The double is the highest domino of each suit, followed in order by the 6, 5, 4, 3, 2, 1, and blank.

A domino whose ends add up to five or a multiple of five is a "count" domino. There are two count tiles worth 10 points each: 5-5 and 6-4. There are three count tiles worth 5 points each: 5-0, 4-1, and 3-2. All 5-count tiles add up to a total of 35 points. A count scores extra points for the team that wins it in a trick.

Bidding continues clockwise around the table, with the shuffler always having the last option to bid. Each player has only one opportunity to bid. The minimum bid is 30. A player must pass if he is unable to bid at least 30 or raise a previous bid. If all 4 players pass, all tiles are returned to the deck and then reshuffled by the player to the left of the last player to shuffle.

The player making the highest bid is the first player and the player to declare which suit is trump for that hand. (A player never reveals the trump suit until he has won the bid and is ready to play the first tile.)

The first player plays a tile from his hand. Play continues to his left. The next three plays made by the other players at the table must "follow suit." This means those three players must play a tile that is of the same suit as the highest end of the first tile played in that trick, unless the first player plays a tile with at least one end from the same suit as what was declared "trumps" for that hand. In that case, the next three plays made must be a tile with an end from the trump suit.

For example, if the 6-4 is played first, the other players would have to follow suit with a 6 from their own hand. But if either end of the first tile played is of the trump suit, then the trump overrides the other number and everyone must follow suit with a trump.

If a player holds more than one playable tile in his hand, he may play any one of them. If a player is unable to follow suit because he does not hold that suit in his hand, he may play any tile from his hand, even a trump.

The player who plays the highest tile of the lead suit or the highest trump wins the trick. The winner of each trick plays the first tile for the next trick, at which time he may play any tile in his hand.

When all four players have each played one tile, these four tiles are collectively a trick. There are seven tricks in each hand. Each trick is worth one point.

One player from each team should collect all the tricks for that team, regardless of which player won the trick. After each trick has been won, the tiles should be moved to one side or corner of the table, the 4 tiles side by side and faceup. This simplifies scoring.

Once all 7 tricks have been played, each team should total their number of tricks (1 point per trick) and their total number of points on count dominoes collected (5 and multiples of 5), respectively.

If the bidding team makes or exceeds their bid, then that team receives credit for all the points they won during that hand. In that case, the opponents also receive credit for any points they won during the hand.

For example: If a team bids 30 and then takes 35 points in the hand, then it has successfully reached its bid and scores 35 points. The opponents receive credit for its 7 points.

If a team fails to reach their bid, then that team scores nothing, and the opposing team receives credit for the original bid they defeated, plus the actual points they won during the hand.

For example: If your team wins the bid at the beginning of the game with a bid of 37 but took only 35 points in the hand, your team would score 0, and the opponents would score 44 points (their 7 points plus your bid of 37 points).

After each hand, the player to shuffle the tiles rotates to the left (clockwise). Play continues in this same manner.

The first team to reach 250 points wins. If both teams reach 250 points on the same hand, the team that made the bid on that final hand is the winner of the game, regardless of the score.

Variation: A simplified scoring system can be used with one "mark," or point, awarded for the victory of a hand. The first team to win 7 marks wins the match.

The instructions given here are probably sufficient for the beginner, but only serve as the basics of the game of Forty-Two. To learn more about the strategy of the game and for a more in-depth description of how the game is played, I suggest you refer to Winning 42: Strategy & Lore of the National Game of Texas," by Dennis Roberson and published by Texas Tech University Press in Lubbock, Texas, in 1997. The book also includes interesting information about the history of the game that I found to be very enjoyable reading.

SET VARIATIONS

Each of the following four games is a variation of the game of Forty-Two and each is played with two sets of double-6 dominoes. As a general rule, Eighty-Eight is the only game of the four that requires leading with a trump. When the game rules call for a player to lead with a trump, the game becomes more challenging.

Use this rule when playing the following games any time there are tiles in the boneyard after a hand is drawn: The highest bidder looks at the tiles in the boneyard. If one or both of the dominoes are count dominoes, the bidder must take the one or two count dominoes into his hand and remove the same number of tiles from his hand. Therefore, there will still be two tiles in the bone-

yard but neither will be a count domino. He should make this exchange of tiles without showing the tiles to any other player at the table.

Use the rules to Forty-Two, with the following variations.

Seventy-Nine

Domino set: Two sets of double-6 dominoes.
Number of players: 6, playing as two teams of 3 players per team.
Number of dominoes drawn: Each player draws 9 tiles. This leaves 2 tiles remaining in the boneyard. The minimum bid is 50.

There are 9 tricks and each trick is worth one point.

Total of 79 points to be won in each hand: 70 (35 points in a double-6 set × 2 sets) + 9 (9 tricks at 1 point each) = 79.

Eighty

Domino set: Two sets of double-6 dominoes; remove all blank tiles.

Number of players: 4 players play as two teams of 2 players per team.

Number of dominoes drawn: Each player draws 10 tiles. This leaves 2 tiles remaining in the boneyard. The minimum bid is 60.

There are 10 tricks and each trick is worth 2 points.

Total of 80 points to be won in each hand: 60 (30 points in a double-6 set with 7 blanks removed from the set × 2) + 20 (10 tricks at 2 points each) = 80.

Eighty-Four

Domino set: Two sets of double-6.

Number of players: 8 players play as two teams of 4 players per team or 6 players play as two teams of 3 players per team.

Number of dominoes drawn: When 8 play, each

player draws 7 tiles and there are no tiles remaining in the boneyard. When 6 play, each player draws 9 tiles with 2 tiles remaining in the boneyard.

The minimum bid is 60.

With 8 players, there are 7 tricks and each trick is worth 2 points. With 6 players, there are 9 tricks and each trick is worth 2 points.

Total of 84 points to be won in each hand:

With 8 players: 70 (35 points in a double-6 set × 2) + 14 (7 tricks at 2 points each) = 84.

With 6 players: 70 (35 points in a double-6 set × 2) + 0 (tricks are worth nothing when playing this game with 6 players) + 14 (each double is worth one point when playing this game with 6 players) = 84.

Eighty-Eight

Domino set: Two sets of double-6.

Number of players: 6 players play as two teams with 3 players per team.

Number of dominoes drawn: Each player draws 9 tiles. This leaves 2 tiles remaining in the boneyard. The minimum bid is 60.

There are 9 tricks and each trick is worth 2 points.

Total of 88 points to be won in each hand: 70 (35 points in a double-6 set × 2 sets) + 18 (9 tricks at 2 points each) = 88.

BIDDING VARIATIONS

The following bidding variations to the game of Forty-Two rely on the luck of the draw and make it possible for players to score more points with less skill and strategy.

Nel-O

The object of a Nel-O bid is to take no tricks. A Nel-O bidder's hand contains tiles so low he believes his opponents will be unable to force him to take a trick. If Nel-O is the winning bid, players must follow suit of the tile that is led on each trick, and there are no trumps.

When a player bids Nel-O, his partner must turn

the tiles in his hand facedown on the table until the end of the hand, while the bidder plays out the hand with the opposing team. The bidder leads with the first tile. The opponents follow suit of the higher number of that tile. The player who wins the trick is in the lead. For the remainder of the hand, the goal of the opponents is to play lower tiles than the bidder. The bidder is set if he takes one trick.

Some Nel-O players treat doubles as a separate suit, with every player following suit with a double if a double is led. Most, however, do not play by this rule.

Plunge

The tactic of bidding Plunge allows for communication between partners during bidding and start of play about the tiles they hold in their hand. Once play begins, however, the hand plays out just like any regular Forty-Two hand.

If Plunge is the winning bid, the bidder's hand must contain at least four doubles and, by bidding

Plunge, the bidder relays to his partner that he holds a great hand. The bid is automatically 168, and the bidder cannot lose a single trick. The bidder's partner is required to declare trumps, based on his own hand, and to lead by playing the first tile of the first trick.

When a player bids Plunge, he is gambling that he holds the double in his hand to the trumps and offs that his partner has yet to declare. The bidder takes a huge risk by bidding Plunge. If he is lucky, he and his partner match each other on most of the doubles and offs suits; if not, the consequence of his bid is a huge loss.

Sevens

Sevens is a bidding option that has no trumps or suits. The only thing that matters is the total sum of pips on the face of each tile in a bidder's hand. A player bidding Sevens believes he has more tiles in his hand whose pips total 7, or close to 7 (6 or 8), than any other player.

The bidder must bid at least 42 and cannot lose a single trick. The bidder plays his first tile, adding up to 7. Every other player must play a tile from his hand whose pips total 7 or the next-closest sum to 7. On each trick, every player must play the tile left in his hand whose pips total 7 or the tile whose pips total the closest to 7. A player does not have the option of saving that tile for play later in the hand. Play continues in this way. As tricks are played, they should remain in the middle of the table.

To set the bidder, at any point during a hand one of the opponents must play a tile whose total pips are closer to seven than the bidder's. A tie does not set the bidder.

Moon

In this game, bidding starts at 4 tricks and goes as high as 7, called "shooting the moon." There are only 3 players, and each bids or passes once. They can bid 7 or 21: 21 being the game. Failing costs the bidder the points/tricks he or she bid. The opponents get points for the tricks they captured. Tricks are 1 point.

All tiles with blanks, except only the double-blank, are removed from a double-6 set, leaving 22 tiles. Players each draw 7 tiles. The extra is the "widow" for the bidder's hand. If the tile is used, the bidder discards another tile. Moon plays like 42, but with no "count" or partners. Pips are used as suits, with the double being highest.

Games for One Player

In each of the following games, shuffle the tiles, facedown, before drawing your hand. It is important to be consistent in the manner in which you flip each tile over, from facedown to faceup. Choose which way you will turn tiles over and use that method throughout the game.

Fair Lucy

Domino set: Double-6.
Object of the game: To discard all the tiles in the set, two at a time, in pairs whose pips total 12.
Keeping the tiles facedown, draw 7 from the deck

ce them facedown in a horizontal row in
 you. Draw 7 more tiles and, still keeping
all tiles facedown, place one tile on top of each of
the other 7 tiles. Draw 7 more tiles, and do the
same. You should now have 7 stacks of tiles, each
3 tiles high. Now, take the remaining 7 undrawn
tiles and place them faceup, one on top of each of
the 7 stacks.

If any two faceup tiles have pips that together
total 12, discard that pair of tiles. Then turn the
tiles underneath the tiles that were just discarded to
a faceup position. Continue this process of
discarding pairs of tiles whose sum totals exactly
12.

If you play the bottom tile of the stack, leaving
fewer than 7 stacks of tiles, you may not move a
tile to this "empty" spot to create a new stack.

At no time during the game should you have
more than 7 tiles faceup.

Luzon

Domino set: Double-6.

Object of the game: To discard all the tiles in the set, two at a time, in pairs whose pips total 12.

Keeping the tiles facedown, place them in 5 vertical rows of 5 tiles each. Set aside the 3 remaining tiles.

Turn each tile faceup, keeping them in their same positions. If the sum of the pips on any two tiles on the bottom horizontal row totals 12, discard that pair of tiles. The two lower tiles of the same vertical row may not be discarded at one time, even if their pips total 12.

The 3 tiles that were set aside at the beginning of the game may be used at any time during the game, as the player so chooses, to be coupled with any tile from the bottom of a vertical row.

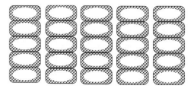

In the course of the game you may end up with less than 5 vertical rows. If this occurs, it is permissible to move a tile from the bottom of any other vertical row in order to form another vertical row. At no point in the game, however, should there be more than 5 vertical rows. This rule is very important because if the 6-5 and the 0-1 or the 6-6 and the 0-0 were in the same vertical row it would be impossible to win without being able to move one of the two tiles to another vertical row.

This is a game of luck and skill. When you make a careful study of your exposed tiles, you will learn that some moves are much better than others.

Polka Dots

(aka Twelves)

Domino set: Double-6.

Object of the game: To discard all the tiles in the set two at a time, in pairs, when pips total 12.

Draw 6 tiles from the deck and place them faceup in a horizontal row in front of you.

If any two tiles in your tableau together have

pips totaling exactly 12, remove those two tiles from your row and set them aside. Then, replace them by drawing two more tiles from the shuffled deck. Continue to do this, and win the game by discarding every tile in the deck.

If the situation arises that there is more than one pair of tiles whose pips total exactly 12, you may discard each and every pair of tiles before replacing your tableau with more tiles from the deck.

If a tile's pips can be added to more than one other tile in the tableau to get a total of 12 pips (for example: a 3-3 can be added to the 6-0 to total 12, or the 3-3 can be added to the 2-4 to total 12), you may discard any pair you choose.

Variations: (1) Use a tableau of 5 tiles for a more difficult game or a tableau of 4 tiles for an even more difficult game. You may also increase the number of tiles in your tableau to 7 for an easier game. (2)

With adjustments, this game can be played with a set of dominoes other than the double-6 set. When playing with a double-9 set, the pips on two tiles in the tableau must total 18 in order to be discarded. The game may be played in this way with any set of dominoes. Just take the total number of pips on the highest tile in the set (for example: 6 for a set of double-3 dominoes; 24 for a set of double-12 dominoes) and that is the number that two tiles in your tableau must total in order to be discarded.

VARIATION FOR FAIR LUCY, LUZON, AND POLKA DOTS

In the regular game, the 0-0 and the 6-6, and the 1-0 and the 6-5, must be matched to make 12, because there is no other way to match them. For the other tiles there are at least two ways each tile can be matched. Therefore, the 1-6 can be matched with the 4-1, 2-3, or 0-5. The game becomes much more difficult if you limit more of the tiles to only one possible match each. Try this variation: Require that each of the ends of the matching pair must total six.

The four remaining tiles (0–6, 1–5, 2–4, and 3–3) are tiles with 6 pips each and cannot be matched to another tile in the set so that the ends of the matching pair of tiles would total six. Therefore, the requirement that the ends of the matching pair of tiles total six will not apply to these four tiles; each of these four tiles may be matched with any one of the other three tiles to make a total of 12 pips for the pair, as in the original game.

Baronet

Domino set: May be played with any set of dominoes.
Object of the game: To remove all the dominoes from the line.

Keeping the tiles facedown, line them all up, side by side, in front of you.

Playing from left to right, with the first domino in the line considered the starting point, turn the dominoes faceup, one at a time, while counting "zero, one, two,...." as each domino is turned faceup.

If the number spoken matches the total sum of the pips on that domino, remove that domino from the line. Continue counting where you left off, as you turn the next domino in line.

Counting begins with zero and ends with the number of pips on the highest double of the set of dominoes you are using for play (double-6: 12; double-7: 14; double-3: 6; double-9: 18; double-12: 24). If playing with a double-6 set of dominoes, count to 12, then begin counting with the number "zero" while turning the next domino in the line.

When you reach the end of the line, return to the first domino, continuing the count from the end of the line. If the number called on the last domino in line was "one," then "two" should be the number called while turning the first domino in line.

Keep repeating this process until all the dominoes in the line have been removed or until you cannot remove any more dominoes.

The Big Clock

(© 1996 by David Galt)

Domino set: Double-12.

Object of the game: To arrange the 12 double tiles from the set into a circular formation, each double being positioned in the same place as it would appear on a clock face. For example, the 1–1 tile would be placed in the formation in the same location the 1 would appear on a clock face; the 2–2 would be placed where the 2 would appear; and so on.

Remove the double-blank tile from the deck. Shuffle the remaining tiles, facedown. Draw 12 tiles, and then place them, faceup, in a circular shape, placing the first tile at the point that will be considered

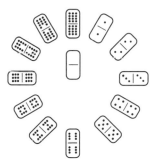

"12:00" (where 12 would appear on a clock face), and continue by placing the second tile at "1:00," and so on, proceeding clockwise. Finally, place the double-blank tile inside your circle, at the very top, so as to "point to 12:00."

After the initial layout is finished, draw tiles one at a time from the deck, seeking to place each tile face up on top of another tile in your clock formation. When placing one tile on top of another, at least one end of the tile you are playing should match at least one end of the tile you are covering.

If you drew the 6-10, you could play it on the 3-10, 6-1, or 4-6.

The best play, however, is likely to be on the 4-6 at the "10:00" time slot, in case you soon draw the 10-10.

By the way, never place a tile on top of a double, whether the double is in its correct time slot or not.

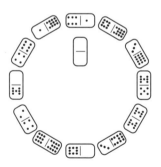

Except when it's a double tile, if you are unable to play the tile drawn from the deck because there is no match, place that tile aside, never to be drawn during the remainder of the game.

When you draw a double that has no match on the clock at all or when you have a double on the clock but in the wrong place, this is called a "double in trouble." The 7-7 at "4:00" in the drawing is a "double in trouble."

When you have a "double in trouble," you may move the top domino of any pile to the top of another pile, as long as at least one end of the tile being moved has the same number of pips as at least one end of the tile it is being placed on top of. Continue making as many such moves as necessary in order to bring any "double in trouble" to its correct time slot. You may even empty an entire time slot in this way, creating a blank space.

If you cannot fill a blank time slot with its correct double, fill it immediately with a new tile.

As soon as you place a double in its correct time slot, turn that tile, along with all the tiles underneath it, so it radiates out.

If you draw a double that cannot be played anywhere, the game is lost.

Variations: This game may be played with a double-9 set, in which case your clock face will not be a complete circle, starting with "1:00" and going only to "9:00."

You may also play this game with a set of double-6 dominoes, using a half-circle for your clock face or dealing the 6 tiles in a straight row, if you prefer.

The Buccaneer

Domino set: Double-6.

Object of the game: To get one of the seven doubles at the bottom of each stack and to have the remaining three dominoes in that stack be of the same suit as the double domino on the bottom of the stack.

Keeping the tiles facedown, place them in seven separate stacks of four dominoes each. Turn faceup

the top domino on each of the seven stacks.

A domino may be moved from one stack to another if the number of pips on one end of the domino being moved matches the number of pips on one end of the domino onto which the move is made.

As the facedown dominoes are uncovered, turn them faceup and leave them on their stack. Never have more than five dominoes in any stack at any time.

If you play the bottom domino of any stack, leaving an "empty space," only a double domino may be used to start a new stack in that space.

Never turn a domino faceup unless it is the only domino in a stack or the top domino of the stack.

Castle Rock

Domino set: May be played with any set of dominoes.
Object of the game: To discard all the dominoes in the set.

Draw 3 tiles from the boneyard and turn them faceup, in a row. For explanatory purposes, let's call these three dominoes, from left to right, "Domino 1," "Domino 2," and "Domino 3."

If the pips on one end of Domino 1 match the pips on one end of Domino 3, then Domino 2 is removed from the row.

Continue to draw dominoes, always adding to the right side, or end, of the row. When a match occurs between the ends of any two dominoes being separated by one domino, the domino between of the matching dominoes is removed from the row.

Also, when a match occurs between the ends of three dominoes in a row, the player has the option of removing all three dominoes from the row. He or she may decide it is not the best strategy to remove all three dominoes, depending on what the situation will be like after either move. However, the player must always remove at least one domino when the opportunity arises.

Should you discard all the dominoes from the array, you simply draw from the stock to start a new array as at the beginning. Keep repeating this process until you have discarded all dominoes in the set or until you cannot discard any more dominoes.

Five-Up Solitaire

Domino set: Double-6. Draw 5 tiles from the deck. Set any tile, and then play as many tiles from your hand as possible. Continue to play using the same rules you would use with 2 or more players.

When playing this game, you may wish to play against the deck, keeping separate scores: one for you and one for the deck. Try these ideas: At the beginning of each hand, give the deck 5 points if you're a beginner and 10 points if you're more experienced. This will offset the scores you will make during play. The deck receives 3 points if you overdraw. If the game ends in block, the deck receives the points left in your hand. If your total score is 61 points or more and you are ahead at the end of that hand, you have won the game. If the deck has a total score of 61 points or more and is ahead at the end of that hand, the deck wins the game.

Good Neighbors

(© 1996 by David Galt)

Domino set: Double-12.

Object of the game: To pair up and remove all the dominoes but one.

Keeping the tiles in a facedown position, draw 12 from the deck and place them in three horizontal rows of 4 tiles per row. Now, turn them faceup in place. This is your tableau.

You may remove from your tableau pairs of tiles that are "good neighbors." "Good neighbors" are tiles that are next to each other (including diagonally) and have matching ends. (At least one end of one tile has to have the same number of pips as at least one end of the other tile.)

On each turn, remove at least one pair of "good neighbors." (You may remove more than one pair if you like.) In this layout, there are several "good neighbor" pairs to choose from: 6-1 + 12-6; 9-12 + 12-6; 9-12 + 12-3; 3-2 + 3-1; 3-2 + 5-3; and 9-3 + 3-1.

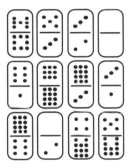

When a pair (or pairs) is removed from your tableau, this leaves empty spaces. All the remaining tiles should be moved towards the upper left-hand corner of your tableau. This is done first by moving any remaining tiles having one or more empty spaces to their left, over to the left, filling in that space (those spaces). Then move tiles from the left-hand side of the middle row up to the right-hand side of the top row and tiles from the left-hand side of the bottom row up to the right-hand side of the middle row. After this is done, draw tiles from the deck and place them in the empty spaces of the tableau, left to right, and top to bottom, making your tableau once again, 3 horizontal rows of 4 tiles per row.

Example: Let's say you remove the 3-2 + 3-1 and 6-1 + 12-6 from your tableau. Move 0-0 over to the left; bring 9-12 up to the top row; move 12-3 to the left; bring the bottom three tiles up one row; pick 4 new tiles from the deck and place them, left to right, on the bottom row.

In this way, pair, remove, and fill-in repeatedly. You lose the game any time you are "stuck" and have no "good neighbors" to remove from your tableau.

Variations: This game may be played with a double-9 set, in which case your tableau should be 3 horizontal rows of 3 tiles per row. The object is to remove all dominoes but one when playing with a double-9 set.

Or you may play this game with a set of double-6 dominoes, with a tableau of two horizontal rows of 6 tiles per row. The object when playing with a double-6 set is to remove all dominoes.

The Jubilee

Domino set: Double-6.

Object of the game: To transfer all the tiles from the several stacks to a particular formation of tiles.

Keeping the tiles in a facedown position, draw 7 from the deck and place them in a horizontal row in front of you with sides touching.

Draw 6 more tiles and, still keeping all the tiles facedown, place one tile on top of each of the other tiles, leaving the far left-hand tile uncovered. Now draw 5 tiles, and add these to the top of each of the other tiles, leaving the two far left-hand tiles uncovered. Now draw 4 tiles, then 3, and so on, continuing to place your tiles, facedown, on top of your horizontal row from right to left.

When done, you should have 7 stacks of tiles, facedown, sides touching, containing the following number of tiles in each stack, from left to right: 1, 2, 3, 4, 5, 6, 7. Turn the tile on top of each stack, 7 in all, faceup.

Only tiles from the top of each stack may be

moved. They may be moved from one stack to another stack or from a stack to the formation shown below. It is permissible for a stack to contain more than 7 tiles during the course of the game; however, there should never be more than 7 stacks at a time.

Any time you have a facedown tile at the top of a stack (this will happen after you have moved a faceup tile in order to make a play), you should turn this tile faceup.

When every tile in a stack is played, leaving an "empty" spot, a new stack may be started in that place—but only with a double, and that double must come from the top of another stack.

It is against the rules to look at any of the tiles that are not already turned faceup at the top of each stack, however.

Patience

(aka Little Harp)

Domino set: Double-6.

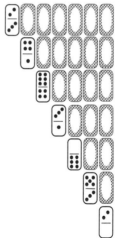

Object of the game: To have all tiles turned faceup in 7 or fewer vertical rows.

Keeping the tiles facedown, place them in 7 rows. The first row contains 7 tiles; the second row contains 6; and so on, each row containing one less tile and the last row containing only one tile. Then, turn the far left tile of each horizontal row faceup.

289

Choose the way you will turn tiles over from facedown to faceup and use that method consistently throughout the game.

Move the faceup tiles from one row to another, placing matching end to matching end, without turning the tile around.

Any time you have a facedown tile at the end of a row (this happens after you have moved a faceup tile in order to make a play), you should turn this tile faceup.

In the course of the game you may end up with less than 7 vertical rows. If this occurs, it is permissible to move a tile or a full or partial horizontal row of matching tiles, in order to

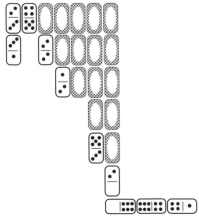

form another vertical row. At no point in the game, however, should there be more than 7 vertical rows.

Squeeze

(© 1996 by David Galt)

Domino set: Double-12, double-9, or double-6.
Object of the game: To have no dominoes left at the end of the game. To have one or two dominoes left at the end of the game is considered a very near win.

Keeping the tiles facedown, draw 7 tiles from the deck and place them in a horizontal row in front of you.

You may remove any pair of tiles that have matching ends (at least one end of one tile has to have the same number of pips as at least one end of the other tile) and which are separated by one or two tiles in the tableau. In addition, you may remove any 3 or more tiles in a row that have matching ends. If there is more than one possible play, you may choose which move to make.

After removing tiles from your tableau in this way, just squeeze the remaining tiles in the row closer together. Then remove more tiles from your tableau, if possible, until all possible plays have been made. Once it is not possible to remove any more tiles, draw 7 new tiles from the deck and add them to the end (right side) of the row.

Continue this process of matching, removing, then adding more tiles to your row until you have won the game by removing all tiles from your tableau or until the game is lost because you are unable to remove the remaining tiles in your tableau.

Note: It takes both planning and luck to finish with no tiles left. For your final play, you'll need to have 3 or more tiles in a row with matching ends.

Stack

Domino set: Double-6.

Object of the game: To play all dominoes in the deck by matching them, one at a time, to one of the eight exposed ends in the tableau.

Draw 4 tiles from the deck and place them faceup in a horizontal row in front of you.

Next, draw another tile from the deck. Make a play by matching one end of that tile to one of the eight exposed ends in your tableau. Continue in this manner by drawing tiles, one at a time, from the deck and then matching one end of the tiles to an open end in your tableau.

If at any time there is no match and a play cannot be made, the game is over and you have lost. If you succeed in playing all 28 dominoes, by matching them with another tile in your tableau, you have won the game.

Variations:: For a more challenging game, start by drawing 3 tiles instead of 4. For a less difficult game, draw 5—or even 6—tiles to begin.

The Sultan

Domino set: Double-6.
Object of the game: To discard all the tiles in the row, two at a time, in pairs whose ends, sides touching, match horizontally.

Keeping the tiles in a facedown position, place all the tiles in the deck in a horizontal row in front of you with sides touching. Then turn the tiles over to a faceup position and do not remove them from their original order in the row. Choose which way you will turn tiles over, from facedown to faceup, and use that method consistently throughout the game.

From your row of 28, discard any two tiles that have adjoining ends that match horizontally. Do not discard adjoining tiles with ends that match only vertically.

After discarding a pair of tiles from your row, move the tiles in your row closer together to take up the space in the row and so that all sides of each tile in the row are touching.

This is a game of luck and skill. When you make a careful study of your exposed tiles, you will learn that some moves are much better than others.

Sympathy

Domino set: Double-6.

Object of the game: To discard all but one tile in the set by removing each tile one at a time and leaving only the 6-6 remaining in your tableau at the end of the game.

Draw 4 tiles from the deck and place them faceup in a horizontal row in front of you.

Remove any tile in the tableau that has exactly one pip less than any other tile in the tableau.

Draw 4 more tiles and place them, faceup, on top of the three remaining tiles in your tableau and in the "empty" space of the tile removed with the first play. The tiles underneath other tiles should be completely covered so that none of the pips are showing.

Again, remove any tile in the tableau that has exactly one pip less than any other tile in the tableau, as you did with your first play. Then draw 4 more tiles, and so on, continuing in this same manner throughout the game. If at any point in the game there is more than one play that could be made, it is usually best to remove the tile with the lowest number of pips.

Traffic

(© 1994 by David Galt)

Domino set: Double–12, double–9, or double–6.
Object of the game: To use up all the tiles by playing them in quads. A *quad* is four consecutive numbers running in ascending or descending order, and

played in a straight line. Blanks count only as 0 in 0-1-2-3.

When playing with a double-6 set, draw 4 tiles; a double-9 set, draw 5; and, a double-12 set, draw 6. Return to this same number of tiles after each turn.

Draw the correct number of tiles from the deck, then place them, faceup, in front of you. Use 2, 3, or 4 of the tiles drawn to make four numbers in a row: a quad. For example, playing with a set of double-6 dominoes, you draw 3-6, 1-2, 2-4, and 5-5. Begin play with a quad of all four tiles or with a quad of three tiles.

Once you have made a quad, leave it in your tableau and continue the process by again drawing the correct number of tiles from the deck.

Continue to draw more tiles from the deck one at a time, attaching enough new tiles to a number played already to make a new quad. But, if at any turn you can't make a quad, you lose. After awhile, your dominoes will start forming a real traffic snarl!

To make a new quad, you will usually add 2 or 3 dominoes. Sometimes you can do it with just one. This must be a domino with consecutive numbers that you can attach in sequence. For instance, you can play 7-6 after 9-8 — or before 5-4 — if either is available.

As long as you make a quad at each turn, other number sequences you make don't matter at all.

Just be sure to observe these don'ts:

- Don't move any dominoes already played.
- Don't make a straight line of five or more numbers in a row. Four is the limit!

Games Using Special Domino Sets

The games in this section are played with special sets of dominoes. Four of the games—Doublecross, Pip, Spinner, and Wildstar—are played with a set of dominoes that includes 55 tiles (a double-9 set of dominoes) plus wild tiles and/or directional tiles that come with the game.

The game of Spoiler is played with a special 48-tile set, with "link" and "dead end" tiles, and a hexagon starter piece. A center starter piece is also included with the games of Pip and Wildstar.

The RaceHorse game uses a special 28-tile set of dominoes with numerals instead of pips.

Doublecross

(© 1990 by Gamesource)

Domino set: 48 playing tiles; one score pad.

Object of the game: To be the first player or team to accumulate 500 points.

Number of tiles drawn: If 2 or 3 play, each draws 12 tiles; 4 or 5 play, each draws 9; and if 6 play, each draws 8 tiles. (If 6 play, there will be no remaining tiles after the draw, therefore, there will be no drawing during the game.)

Place all the tiles facedown and shuffle.

The player with the triple-6 tile begins the round by placing the tile faceup on the playing surface. If the triple-6 is not drawn, the next-highest triple starts the round.

The play proceeds in a clockwise manner.

If a player is unable to place a tile from his hand, he draws one tile from the draw pile.

If a player is still unable to place a tile, play passes to the next player.

Each round ends when any player plays all the tiles in his hand. All other players add up their remaining tiles, and those points are awarded to the winner of the round.

In team play, only the opposing team's points are added to the winning team's score.

Scoring:

QUAD SCORE: Player matches one or two sections of a tile to form a quad. Point value: 12 points.

DOUBLE QUAD SCORE: Player matches two sections to form two quads. Point value: 22 points.

BRIDGE SCORE: A tile is used to connect the ends of two existing tiles. Point value: 6 points.

T-BRIDGE SCORE: A tile is placed using the middle section and only one end to match an existing pattern. Point value: 20 points.

DOUBLE SCORE: Player matches a tile that forms one quad and two additional sections. Point value: 30 points.

TRIPLE SCORE: Occurs only when a tile is placed

parallel to an existing pattern and all 3 sections match. Point value: 28 points.

DOUBLECROSS: Player places a triple tile to match an existing pattern. The point value of a doublecross is the sum × 2. Point value: 24 × 2 = 48 points!

Note: The first score occurs when the first quad is formed.

Pip

(© 1991 by Michael Poor)

Domino set: The game is played with a special set of dominoes that includes a double-9 set (55 pieces), plus 11 wild "pip" tiles, 4 directional tiles (S, R, A, D) with wild "pip" ends, for a total of 70 tiles, and 1 game-starter center piece.

Directional tiles may be used at any time to create strategic plays. They are:

"S" (skip tile): Play skips the next player.

"R" (reverse tile): Reverses the direction of play.

"A" (play-again tile): Allows that player an additional turn.

"D" (draw tile): Forces the next player to draw

an additional tile from those remaining in the stock pile. If no stock pile is available, the player using the draw tile passes a tile from his hand to the next player.

Each directional tile also has a wild pip design at its opposite end which is wild and may be played as any number.

Wild-pip tiles: There are 11 wild-pip tiles, which may be played as any number. The wild double-pip tile must be played as a double number only.

Number of players: 2 or more.

Object of the game: To be the player with the lowest score after nine rounds of play.

Choose one player to be the scorekeeper. Keeping the tiles facedown on the table, each player draws 9 tiles from the deck. The remaining tiles comprise the stock pile. With 2 players only, each draws 15 tiles.

The player with the 1-1 tile (or the double "pip" tile in the event the 1-1 is not drawn) begins the round by placing it faceup in the center slot of the wooden center piece. If the double-pip tile is used to

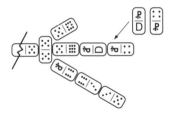

begin any round, it will represent the number tile for that round. (For example: Round 4 begins with the 4-4 tile or the double-pip tile. If the double-pip tile is used to begin that round, it represents the 4-4 tile.) Each round begins with the double tile next in value (e.g., double-2, 3, 4, 5, progressing through 9). There are nine rounds in a game.

If neither the 1-1 nor the double-pip tile is drawn, the designated scorekeeper draws one tile from the stock pile. Each player continues to draw from the stock pile in a clockwise manner until the 1-1 or the double-pip tile is drawn.

Play proceeds in a clockwise manner.

The second player may play on either side of the starting tile, using a 1 or a wild-pip tile, placing it horizontally against the first tile played.

The third and all subsequent players may place their tile on either the unplayed side of the original domino or on the previously played domino. Players are free to play on either side of any domino (or on the top and bottom of the 1-1 or pip tile) only when both sides of the starting tile have had play.

A player using a double tile places it vertically on the playing surface.

When a double tile is played (except for the initial start-of-the-game play), the next three plays must be played on the double using either a corresponding-number tile or a wild-pip tile. Play may then proceed from any "branch" on the playing surface.

If a player is unable to place a tile from his hand, he draws one tile from the stock pile. If he is still unable to place a domino, play passes to the next person.

The round is over when a player has played all the tiles in his hand or when a round is blocked. A round is blocked when no player can place a tile from his hand, and the stock pile has been depleted.

When the round is over because a player has played all the tiles in his hand, that player is considered the winner for that round. In the case of the round ending in a block, all tiles remaining in each player's hand are counted and added to their scores. There is no winner for that round, and no player may deduct any points from his score.

Scoring: At the end of every round, each player totals the count of each tile remaining in his hand. Count is determined by the total number of pips of each tile, in addition to the points from any wild tiles as follows:

Single wild-pip tiles count 20 points each, plus the number of dots on the tile.

Double wild-pip tiles count 50 points each.

Each directional tile counts as 25 points, not including the "pips" on the tile which are an additional 20 points. The points are totaled, and the scorekeeper records each player's total. The scorekeeper then deducts 10 points from the round winner's score.

Note: No player's score may fall below zero.

RaceHorse

(© 1990 by Ferman C. Rice)

The creator of this game, Ferman Rice, said, "The reason the game is called RaceHorse is because you can come back from the stretch to the lead in a short period of time. It's a game that when you are down, you don't have to despair."

Domino set: The game is played with a special 28-tile set of dominoes bearing numerals instead of pips. These tiles are called "horses."

Number of players: 2 to 4 players.

Object of the game: To be the first player to earn a score of 250.

Shuffle the tiles face (numbered side) down. Then, each player draws one tile from the deck. The player who turns over the horse with the highest number gets to play first. After this, play rotates back and forth or around the table.

After reshuffling the tiles, each player draws his hand from the deck.

Number of dominoes drawn: For 2 players, 7 horses each; for 3 players, 6 horses each; for 4, 5 horses each. The remaining horses are set aside to be drawn as needed. This game is basically the game of Five-Up, with some additions.

Set: Any domino may be used as set.

Each player tries to match the number on one end of a tile from his hand with the number on an open end of any tile in the layout. Color coding simplifies this.

A player is awarded points every time he makes a play that results in the open ends of the tiles in the line of play adding up to a multiple of 5. (5 points for 5 pips; 10 points for 10 pips; 15 points for 15 pips; and so on.) Each player must announce his points on making his play in order to receive credit for the points made. The player who dominoes is also awarded points at the end of each hand by adding up, and rounding to the nearest multiple of 5, the pips on the tiles left in his opponents' hands.

When a player scores, he must play again until he can no longer score. At that point, he plays one more tile before it becomes the other player's turn. Scores must be counted after each play.

Horses with double numbers are called "daily doubles"; when played, they entitle the player to play again. Points on the ends of the daily doubles count only after they have been played on—unless they are a dead end.

A play cannot be made on the end of a daily double until after plays have been made on both sides—unless it dead ends.

When a player cannot play, he must draw a horse. If he still cannot play, he must keep drawing until he can. If he scores, he must play again, or draw until he can play.

In the event a player can't play, and there are no more horses left to draw, he must pass his turn to the next player.

If a player plays a scoring tile or a daily double,

he must draw until he can play again.

The first player to play his last horse gets to keep the points left in his opponent's hand and adds them to his score, rounding to the nearest 5 points.

If the first horse you play is a 5 or 10 tile, or may be added together with the open ends of the layout to total 5 or 10 points, you receive those points and play again.

Only the points on the ends of the horses count.

There are no "9" dominoes in the game. Be careful not to mistake the "6" tile for a "9."

Spinner™

(© 1997 by Gamesource, 1983
by Dr. James F. & Edna Graham)

Domino set: The game is played with a special set of dominoes that includes a full set of double-9 dominoes plus 11 extra "spinner" dominoes, for a total of 66 domino tiles.

Number of players: 2 to 8 players.

Object of the game: To be the player with the lowest score.

Number of dominoes drawn: If 2 players, draw 14 dominoes each. If 3 to 8 players, draw 7 dominoes each. The remaining domino tiles make up the boneyard.

Spinners are wild.

Set: The first domino played must be the 9-9 or a double-spinner as a substitute for the 9-9. If no player has a 9-9 or double-spinner, the player who shuffled the dominoes draws one domino from the boneyard. Play continues to the left, each player drawing one domino from the boneyard until a 9-9 or double-spinner is drawn and then set.

Once the 9-9 or double-spinner is drawn, it is placed in the center of the table. The second and third play must be a 9 or a wild spinner. Players must draw one domino from the reserve pile each time they do not have a domino to play from their hand.

After each double is played, the next 3 plays must be placed on that double. The tiles played on the double must have either a matching end to the double in the layout or a spinner. Each player who does not have a tile with a matching end or a spinner must draw 1 domino from the reserve pile. Unless a domino is drawn that will play, the player passes.

Upon completion of 3 dominoes played on the double, the following player is free to play on any end of the layout—either matching the end domino or playing a spinner. Play your large domino if possible; this will stop the next player from discarding a large double.

Continue play until one player wins the hand by playing all the dominoes in his or her hand. The pips plus spinners are counted on all unplayed dominoes left in each player's hand at the end of each hand. Each player gives the total number to the scorekeeper.

Continue the game by starting the next hand with the 8-8 tile or the double-spinner; the following hand with the 7-7 or the double-spinner; and so on, the last hand beginning with the 0-0 as set domino.

The winner of the previous hand always shuffles for the next hand and is the first player to draw from the boneyard if no player holds the correct double to set or a double-spinner.

At the end of each game, add each player's total score. The player with the lowest score is the winner.

Players may agree, prior to the start of any game, to play a shorter game. To shorten the game, in the first round the player holding the 9-9 sets. If no one holds the 9-9, the player holding the 8-8 sets. If no one holds the 8-8, the player holding the 7-7 sets, and so on.

Spoiler

(© 1994 by David W. Crump)

David Crump had been in the toy, hobby, and game business for a good many years as a retailer before creating Spoiler. He has also designed credits for several military simulation games. Spoiler was created while driving between his game stores in Dallas, Texas. First, the idea of the hexagon starter piece came to mind. Next, while approaching the tollbooth of the North Dallas Tollway, the "dead end" piece was envisioned. The game also incorporates the "link," or wild card, common in many games. The special doubles play evolved in play testing. Credit for the game's title goes to David's wife, Rosanne. It was her idea to call the piece with both a "link" and a "dead end" a "spoiler" because it spoils an opponent's upcoming play.

Domino set: A special 48-tile set, with "link" and "dead end" tiles, and a hexagon starter piece.

Object of the game: To be the first to earn a score of at least 100 points times the number of players.

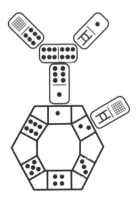

(For example: If there are 4 players, the winning score is 400 points or more.)

Spoiler is played in rounds. In each round, you try to get rid of all your tiles first. Branch your "doubles" and play an extra domino on each of the doubles in your same turn. Block your opponents' moves with the special "dead end." Use your dominoes with link ends when you are stuck. The quicker you are out of tiles, the more dominoes everyone else will have left in their hand and the larger your score will be.

Mix all the dominoes facedown. The first player

is determined by drawing a single domino. The player who draws the highest value domino (see "Scoring" for values) plays first. The first player of each subsequent round rotates one player to the left (clockwise).

For games with 4 to 6 players, the dominoes are dealt out equally to each player. For games of 2 or 3 players, deal 12 tiles per player. In both cases, set aside any remaining tiles.

Play begins with the hexagon placed in the center of the table. The round's first player makes either a normal play or a special play (see "Special Plays") using any side of the hexagon. A normal play is made by placing a domino end to end with a side of the hexagon or any domino that has a matching end. Play continues to the left with each player making a normal play, a special play, or passing. A player without any legal move must pass.

Special plays: A "link" is a domino end with an inter-locked chain symbol. This special end will link with any domino end except the "dead end." A domino with only one "link" cannot be used as a "double."

A "double link" can be used like any double and new branches created from it (see "Doubles").

A "dead end" is a domino end with a brick wall symbol. A dead end will not connect to any other end and blocks further play on the branch. A deadend is played with the other end matched to the branch. There is no "double dead end."

The "spoiler" is a domino that has both a link and a dead end (a link on one end and a dead end on the other end). This special domino allows you to put a stop to play on any branch but is worth 20 points if you're caught with it in your hand at the end of a round.

Doubles: A "double" is a domino with identical ends. A double can be played like any domino by matching it end to end, but it can also be used for "branching," by matching it sideways to a matching end. A double used to branch is first played sideways and then the player has the option, during the same turn, of playing an additional domino on each end of the new branch. These additional dominoes are positioned at 45-

degree angles to the double's ends and pointed away from the center hexagon. This is a very advantageous play, particularly if you can play all three dominoes.

A round ends when no player has a legal play, all players pass (whether they have a legal play or not), or when a player "goes out" by playing his last domino.

At the end of each round, a winner is determined and a score for the winner is calculated.

Scoring: If a player is the first player to play the last tile in his hand, he is automatically the winner and wins all the points of all remaining dominoes in his opponents' hands.

If the round ends because all players pass or have no legal plays, then the winner is the player with the lowest point value of dominoes remaining in his hand at the end of the round. In this case, the winner receives the points of all unplayed dominoes of the other players less the points of his own unplayed dominoes.

In the unlikely event that more than one player

has the same low score (a tie), then they are co-winners. The points of the unplayed dominoes of all other players are totaled and split (rounded up) between the co-winners. Next, they subtract their own points for their final score (minimum score of 1).

The point value of each domino is the number of dots on both ends. The special dead end and link ends are valued at 10 points each.

Spoiler variations: For a shorter game, play to a winning score of 50 points per player. A normal game of Spoiler plays in about 2 hours, depending on the number of players. The shorter game plays in about an hour.

To play with more players (up to 8 players), combine two sets of Spoiler and play in this way: Each player is dealt 12 tiles with remaining tiles set aside. The winning score is 50 points times the number of players. (For example: If 7 are playing, the winning score is 350 points or more.) You will need a large table.

Wildstar

(© 1995 by Plastech Industries)

Domino set: Game is played with a special set of dominoes that includes a double-9 set (55 pieces) plus 5 extra dominoes, "wildstars," for a total of 60 dominoes and a center starter piece.

Object of the game: To be the first player to dispose of all your dominoes.

Number of players: 2 to 8 players.

First, shuffle the dominoes, facedown, at the beginning of the game. Then each player draws his hand.

Number of dominoes drawn: If 2 players, draw 20 dominoes each. If 3 to 5 players, draw 10 dominoes each. If 6 to 8 players, draw 7 dominoes each. The remaining dominoes make up the boneyard.

After drawing the needed dominoes at the beginning of each hand, the remaining tiles are set aside to be drawn as needed by the players. This is called the "draw pile." For players' convenience, there may be more than one "draw pile" on the table with each player free to draw from any pile.

All wildstar dominoes are wild and can be substituted for any domino—blank through 9—in horizontal or vertical direction, with these two exceptions:

- The double star (wildstar) may not be used as a center domino.
- The five dominoes played around the center must be matching-numbered dominoes—no wildstar. Star dominoes then may be used on all later plays.

The count: Each dot on a domino counts 1 point. (Example: The 6-5 counts 11 points.)

Each wildstar counts 20 points. 0-0 counts 30 points.

The first play of the first round begins with the 9-9 tile. The player holding the 9-9 places that tile in the star center piece to begin the game. Each hand thereafter begins with the next-lowest number double tile. (For example: The first hand begins with the 9-9; the second with the 8-8; and so on, continuing down through the 0-0.)

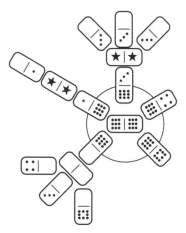

If no player holds the correct double to begin that round, then the person who shuffled the dominoes draws a domino from the "pile." If the shuffler does not draw the correct double, then the drawing continues around the table until one is drawn.

Once the first play of that round has been made, play continues clockwise around the table. The next five plays must be made with tiles that have an end with the same number as the center tile. If a player cannot make a play on the center tile, he must draw a tile from the pile. If the player draws a playable tile, then he may play it. If not, that tile is added to the player's hand and play moves on to the next person.

Once five matching dominoes have been played on the center tile, a player may play any domino from his hand whose end matches the open end of a domino played on the table. A player also has the option of playing a double domino or wildstar domino.

The first player to play all his or her dominoes is the winner of the hand. The other players determine the count of the dominoes remaining in their hands and give their score to the winner of that hand. (See "Partners" if playing as teams.)

In the event the game becomes blocked (no player can make a play), everyone makes a count of their dominoes and that score is added to each person's score or each team's score.

The person winning the previous hand shuffles the tiles for the next hand, and is the first player of the next round.

At the end of the game, the person or team with the lowest score is the winner.

Partners: If an even number of people are playing, they may divide into two teams, sitting alternately around the table. When a member of one team plays the last domino in his hand, only the dominoes left remaining in the hands of the other team are counted and recorded.

Games Using
Oriental Dominoes

All the games in this category are played with a set of Oriental Dominoes, sometimes called Chinese Dominoes. Oriental, or Chinese, domino sets differ from Western, or European, dominoes in several ways.

There are 32 tiles in a set of Oriental dominoes (as opposed to a European double-6 set of 28 tiles); there are no blank ends; 11 of the tiles are duplicated; and most Oriental dominoes are larger than their European counterparts. Oriental sets containing up to 141 tiles are known, but the extra tiles are duplicates of the basic 21. If you were to take a European double-6 set of dominoes and remove all the blank tiles, then duplicate 11 of the tiles (6-6; 6-5; 6-4; 6-1; 5-5; 5-1; 4-4; 3-3; 3-1; 2-2; and 1-1), you would have an Oriental set.

All Oriental dominoes—Chinese, Korean, Burmese, and Thai—consist of 21 pieces representing all the possible throws of a pair of 6-sided

dice. Oriental dice have the ones and fours marked with red pips instead of black, and Oriental dominoes are marked in the same way. In addition, three of the pips at each end of the 6-6 tile are red, though the 6 pips of the corresponding dice are black. These red pips are important in some games. Also, the pip on the end of a tile from the one suit is larger than the pips on the other dominoes and dice.

The names of the various pairs of domino tiles (for example: Supreme, Heaven, Earth, and Man) are the same as the names of the various combinations that can be tossed with a pair of dice.

The 11 pairs of duplicate tiles (22 tiles) in the Oriental set seen at left make up what is called the "civil" series; the remaining 10 non-duplicate tiles in the set form what is called the "military" series.

Bullfighting

(Tau ngau)

Additional equipment: 1 pair of dice to be thrown at the start of the round to determine the "banker."

Object of the game: To beat the bull.

Number of players: 3 to 6 players.

Any number of onlookers may place stakes alongside those of a player of their choice.

Dice are thrown to determine the banker.

The dominoes are shuffled, facedown. Keeping the tiles facedown, each player, including the banker, draws five dominoes. Before looking at their tiles, the players place their stakes in front of them to any limit which may be imposed by the banker. When the stakes have been placed, the players look at their tiles. The value of each tile depends upon its number of pips, except that the 2-1 and 4-2 tiles each may count as 3 points or 6 points.

Every player must discard 3 tiles from his hand which, when added together, total 10, 20, or 30 points. Examples:

3-1 + 2-2 + 1-1 = 10

6-6 + 3-3 + 1-1 = 20   (a multiple of 10)

2-1 + 6-5 + 3-3 = 20   (the 2-1 counting
                          as 3 points)

2-1 + 4-4 + 3-3 = 20   (the 2-1 counting
                          as 6 points)

After discarding 3 tiles, the 2 remaining tiles in each player's hand are exposed. Each player counts the pips on the two exposed tiles and receives a score of 1 point for each pip. In the case when their score is 10 points or more, the first digit of that number is removed. For example, 12 pips would count as 2.

If a player's score is less than the banker's, he loses his stake to the banker; if his score is more than the banker's, the banker pays him the equivalent of his stake. If a player and the banker have equal scores, there is no exchange between them.

If a player cannot discard 3 tiles to form 10 points, or a multiple of 10, he is "stuck," in which case the banker takes his stake. If the banker is "stuck," he pays the equivalent stake to all the players who are able to discard 3 tiles—and not to any players who are "stuck."

When a banker scores points, the player on his right becomes the new banker for the next round. If the banker is "stuck," he remains banker for another round.

After each round, all 32 tiles are shuffled together and then each player draws 5 tiles and the game continues as before.

Collecting Tens

(K'ap t'ai shap)

Popular in Chinese gambling houses in the U.S., this game and one called Playing Heavens and Nines (Ta t'in kau) were the forerunner of the tile game Mah-jongg, which swept the Western World in the 1920s.

Domino set: Many sets of Oriental dominoes are used.

Additional equipment: 4 dice and a cup.

Number of players: 2 or more.

Object of the game: To be the first player to collect 10 tiles consisting of a matching pair of two identical tiles, and four decimal pairs, the sum of the pips of each pair being 10 or a multiple of 10.

Tiles are carefully mixed by the players and piled facedown, 5 tiles high, in a long "woodpile" down the center of the table. At the start of the game, all players place equal wagers in a box on the table. The house takes 5% of the total; the rest goes to the winning player.

The croupier or one of the players shakes 4 dice under a cup, then throws them on the table. That player then counts each player, counterclockwise around the table, starting with the player on his right, and continues to count until he reaches the number thrown. Where the counting ends, that player becomes the leader.

The top tile on the third stack from the end of the pile is removed. The top tile from each alternate stack, up to one less than the number of players, is also removed. These tiles are placed at the far end of the pile.

The leader takes the 2 stacks at the end, containing 10 tiles. The second player on his right takes the next 2 stacks, containing 9 tiles. The remaining players each take 9 tiles.

The players examine their tiles. If the leader has not drawn a winning hand, he discards a tile and places it faceup on the table.

The next player on his right may pick up the tile the first player discarded to complete a winning hand, or he may exchange it for a tile from his hand, which he places faceup on the table. He also draws a tile from the top of the exposed stack of the woodpile. If it does not complete a winning hand, he may either place it faceup on the table or keep it and discard a tile from his hand.

The third player may then take one of the tiles from the table and draw one from the top of the exposed stack. The game continues until one of the

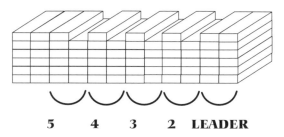

5   4   3   2   LEADER

players wins by collecting 10 tiles: a matching pair of two identical tiles and four decimal pairs, the sum of the pips of each pair being 10 or a multiple of 10. The 2–4 tile only counts as three when making up tens.

The winner of a game takes the contents of the stake box and a new game begins.

Disputing Tens

(Tsung shap)

Object of the game: To be the player with the highest count at the end of the game.

Number of players: 2 players.

The tiles are placed facedown, side by side, in a "woodpile" 4 tiles high and 8 tiles long. The players divide the woodpile between them, each taking 4 stacks. The first player draws the top tile from the stack at the right of his pile and lays it faceup on the table. The second player then draws a tile from his pile and lays it faceup alongside the tile played by the first player. They continue to draw and place the tiles on the table at either end of the row of upturned tiles.

When a tile is played that matches one of the tiles at either end of the row, the player making that play removes both tiles from the row. At the end of the game, they count 10 points for each pip on them.

When a tile is played whose pips make a multiple

of 10 when added to the pips on the tiles at both ends of the row, the player making that play removes the tiles from the row. At the end of the game, each pip on them counts 1 point.

When a tile is played whose pips make a multiple of 10 when added with the pips on the two tiles at either end of the row, the player making that play removes the three tiles from the row.

At the end of the game, each pip on them counts 1 point.

If there are only 2 tiles on the table and a player takes them, he piles them on top of each other to mark a "sweep." A sweep counts 40 points. He then draws from his pile and lays out another tile. If a player fails to take up a winning combination of 2 or 3 tiles, his opponent may take it, then lay out a tile and continue the game.

The game ends when one of the players has played all his tiles.

Fishing

(Tiu u)

Domino set: 2 sets of Oriental dominoes (Each set contains 32 tiles; 2 sets = 64 tiles total.)

Object of the game: To be the player with the highest count at the end of the game.

Number of players: 2, 3, or 4.

Keeping the tiles facedown, place them in 16 stacks of 4 tiles per stack. This is called a "woodpile." If there are 4 players, each player removes 1 stack from one side of the woodpile (4 tiles per player; 16 tiles total). If 3 players, each player removes 2 stacks from one side of the woodpile (8 tiles per player; 24 tiles total). If 2 players, each player removes 3 stacks from one side of the woodpile (12 tiles per player; 24 tiles total).

Take the tiles you have removed from the woodpile and place them faceup.

The players examine their tiles. The first player tries to match one of his tiles with one turned up on the table having the same number of pips. If he is able to find a match, he places the pair faceup in front of him. Whether successful or not, he draws the top tile of the stack at the end of the woodpile from which the last stacks were drawn. Next, he attempts to match that tile with one on the table. If he is able to find a match, he removes the pair. If not, he places the tile drawn with those on the table.

The second player continues in the same way by attempting to match one of his tiles, then drawing a tile from the pile, and so on. The game continues until the pile is exhausted. A pair of 6-6 tiles in a player's hand is laid out at once.

The 2 tiles composing the supreme (2-1 and 4-2) pair with each other and form an exception to the rule in this game that all tiles having the same number of spots pair with each other without reference to their belonging to the civil or military series.

If a player holds a tile in his hand identical with 2 tiles on the table and the fourth tile of the same kind has not been played, he may, at his turn, pile the 3 tiles that are alike one on top of the other, faceup, at the opposite end of the stack from which tiles are being drawn. The player who plays the fourth tile then takes the other three.

When the last tile is drawn, players examine those they have taken. The tiles with 8 or more pips are called large fish and are worth 2 points for each pip of either color. The tiles with fewer than 8 pips are called "minnows" and are worth 1 point for each red pip only. If the score of the minnows is between "tens," round the score up to the higher round number. For example, if the red pips on a player's minnows total 13 points, he earns a score of 20.

The player with the highest count becomes the winner and is paid by each of the players for each point he has in excess of their total.

Pai Gow

(Pai Gow is Cantonese; Pai Jo is Mandarin; aka Pai Kow)
This gambling game is an ancient Chinese or Korean domino game that has become very popular in quite a few Nevada casinos.

Additional equipment needed: 3 dice (to be thrown at the beginning of the game to determine the deal) and a number of chips of varying shapes denoting different denominations (or anything else that can be used for staking). Use chips during the game for staking and then settle accounts at game's end.

Object of the game: To have your high hand beat the banker's high hand and to have your low hand beat the banker's low hand.

Number of players: 4 players (one "banker" and three "punters"); any number of bystanders.

Dominoes are stacked facedown in 2 piles, each pile containing 4 rows of 4 dominoes.

Each player takes a turn throwing 3 dice, going counterclockwise around the table and ending with the player who becomes the first banker, to determine where the deal begins. The dominoes are dealt by the banker, counter-clockwise around the table, each player receiving 4 tiles.

Players examine their tiles without exposing them. From these tiles they form two separate hands of 2 tiles per hand: a high hand and a low hand, each designed to beat the banker's high hand and low hand. When the 3 players have placed their tiles on the table, they put their stake alongside. The banker may impose a limit if he wishes. Any onlooker may participate in the game by placing a stake alongside the tiles of a chosen player.

When all the stakes have been placed, the 3 players expose their first pair, their high hand. Next, the banker exposes his high hand. Then, the players expose their second pair, low hands. The banker follows by exposing his low hand.

To win a round, one of the three players or the banker must win both hands by holding a pair of tiles of higher standing than his opponents. If two different players win one hand each, the round is drawn and stakes are lifted from the table and may be staked again after the next deal. If the banker wins both hands, he takes all the stakes on the table. If a player wins both hands, the banker pays him his stake, and also those of any onlooker who may have laid a stake with him. The banker also pays the other players and participating onlookers, if their pairs rate higher than both of his. If any player's pairs are lower than the banker's, the banker wins their stakes. There is no exchange between banker and a player unless the value of each pair is higher (or lower) on both hands.

When the gains and losses have been settled, the banker deals the second pile of 16 tiles. The second round is played in the same way.

When both rounds are finished, all the tiles are reshuffled and stacked in two piles of 16 dominoes each. The player on the banker's right becomes the new banker, and the game continues. Players may drop out at the end of any round and their place may be taken by an onlooker.

Tien Gow

(aka Tien Kow)

Additional equipment: 1 pair of dice to be thrown at the beginning of the game to determine the banker.
Number of players: 4 players.

A banker is chosen by throwing dice. Eight tiles are dealt to each player by the banker. The players examine their tiles, then the banker leads by placing a tile faceup on the table.

The three players, in turn, follow counterclockwise around the table, each trying to take the trick with a tile of higher value than the others'. If a civil tile is led, the other players must follow with the same suit. If a player is unable to follow suit, he must discard a military tile. Similarly, if a military tile is led, the trick can only be taken by a military tile.

When a player wins the trick, he stacks the tiles in front of him and then leads the next trick with a tile from his hand. The game continues until all 8 tricks have been won.

The player who wins the final trick becomes the new banker and dealer for the next hand. If the banker wins the last trick, he remains banker; but the scoring of the new hand will be different, as described below.

After the last trick of each hand, the points are adjusted, usually by the exchange of counters. Then, the tiles are shuffled, stacked, and dealt by the new banker.

Instead of leading 1 tile, a player may lead 1 of the 16 named pairs or 1 of the 8 pairs comprised of:

6-6 and a mixed 9 (6-3 or 5-4)

1-1 and a mixed 8 (6-2 or 5-3)

4-4 and a mixed 7 (5-2 or 4-3)

3-1 and a mixed 5 (4-1 or 3-2)

The round can only be won by a pair of higher value. The Supreme Couple (2-1 and 4-2) only scores highest when it is led. Otherwise, it is the lowest of the pairs.

If a player wishes, he may lead with two pairs if it is his turn to lead. These can only be captured by two pairs of the same suit, civil or military, and one of the pairs must be of a higher value than either of those led.

Scoring: This is on a basic 4-point system:

- A player with no tricks loses 4 points to the winner of the last trick, who also becomes the new banker.
- A player with fewer than 4 tricks deducts this number from 4 and pays the difference to the winner of the last trick.

- A player winning 4 tricks does not win or lose any points.
- A player winning more than 4 tricks deducts 4 from the number and claims the difference from the winner of the last trick.

If a banker becomes the new banker, the basic figure in the second hand becomes 8 instead of 4; at a third deal, 12; at a fourth, 16; and so on. There is no limit to the number of times a banker may deal. There is usually an indicator on the table to show how many times the banker has dealt. When there is a new banker, the basic figure reverts to 4. Extra points: If the banker leads the Supreme Couple, he claims a bonus of 4 points from each player. If a player leads the Supreme Couple, he claims a bonus of 4 points from the banker and 2 points from each of the other players.

If the banker leads any two of the following couples—6-6 and a mixed nine; 1-1 and a mixed eight; 4-4 and a mixed seven; 3-1 and a mixed five—he claims a bonus score of 8 points from each player. If a player makes the same lead, he wins 8 points from the banker and 4 points from each other player.

A game may finish at a set time or by mutual consent.

Twister: Dragon Dance

(© 1984 by Domino32 Company)

Number of players: 2 to 4 players.

Seven different results have been developed for this new game:

- Tornado: vertical head, vertical tail; head upward.
- Thunderbolt: vertical head, vertical tail; head downward.
- Joy: horizontal head, horizontal tail.
- Wildfire: horizontal head, vertical tail; tail upward.
- Floweret: horizontal head, vertical tail; tail downward.
- Hero: vertical head, horizontal tail; head upward.
- Misfortune: vertical head, horizontal tail; head downward.

Players take turns to place out their dominoes. The strategy is to match domino ends; try to block other players from matching domino ends.

The first domino placed (center, horizontal) is considered to be at the "sun" location.

Whenever a horizontal line reaches a length of 7 dominoes, change direction to vertical on either end. (One end always goes upward, the other downward.)

Decide which vertical direction is "upward;" which is "downward."

Whenever a vertical line reaches a length of 3 dominoes, change direction to horizontal again.

The ever-bending domino line is, of course, always a continuous line.

It is quite difficult to complete a domino32 dragon. All dominoes must be used. Concentrate on the competition; try to win the game. Only when it is an absolute tie, can you have a complete dragon.

You will notice something very interesting: Your dragon surely does have a "head" and "tail" and is alive! At one end, there's a big head, at the other, a split tail. (The head is number (?)! The tail is number is (?)! Try it and find out the two numbers for yourself.)

Believe it or not! You may manipulate domino32 to see if you can ever make a whole dragon without a head or tail at its two ends. Isn't it a strange thing? Traditional domino play of 28 pieces can never do that! Why? Sorry, you'll have to ask a mathematician.

Now you can study what kind of dragon you players, as a group, have made. Check the head and tail numbers so as not to be confused. Remember, there are seven possible dragon-dance forms:

Vertical head, *vertical tail*; *head upward:* This is an evil dragon, a "tornado." Its tail hits the ground, causing great damage.

Vertical head, *vertical tail*; *head downward:* Another evil dragon, a "thunderbolt." You have made an aggressive dragon.

Horizontal head, *horizontal tail:* A peaceful dragon, easy-going and happy. We call it "joy."

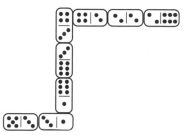

Horizontal head, vertical tail; tail upward: This is a naughty dragon. You build a "wildfire."

Horizontal head, vertical tail; tail downward: What a dandy dragon. Is it a "floweret"?

Vertical head, horizontal tail; head upward: An alert and daring one. This dragon's name is "hero."

Vertical head, horizontal tail; head downward: Unfortunately the dragon is sick. It is a "misfortune."

So you know what kind of team players you are, by observing the twister dance of the whole dragon you have made together, you will find whether your team is a tornado, a thunderbolt, a joy, a wildfire, a floweret, a hero, or a misfortune!

Acknowledgments

Thanks to the following domino book authors (some also domino game creators): R.C. Bell (*Discovering Dice and Dominoes*); Gary M. Grady and Suzanne Goldberg (*Dominoes "Rules of the Games"* series); Lloyd McLeod and the heirs of George McAlister (*Dominoes Texas Style*); Dennis Roberson (*Winning 42: Strategy and Lore of the National Game of Texas*); Mary D. Lankford (*Dominoes Around the World*); and Charles B. Wallace (*Win at Dominoes*). I owe a special thank-you to Victor T. Lewis, who inspired *me* to write my own book on domino games. After contacting his publisher, I searched extensively, to no avail, for Fredrick Berndt, author of *The Domino Book* (Thomas Nelson, 1974). I have included here a few of his games.

Thanks also to the following domino game creators for permission to include their tile games: David Crump; David Galt; Edna Graham; Charles T. Gravley; Betty Howsley at Howsley's Fox Creek Store; Roy and Katie Parsons; Michael Poor at Intellitoy; and Ferman Rice. Thanks also to: Joseph Madachy of *The Journal of Recreational Mathematics*; Cindy Hillman and Kyle McAlister, children of the co-author of *Dominoes Texas Style*; Barbara Brumley, daughter of Lloyd McLeod, co-author of *Dominoes Texas Style*; Fred Armanino, relative of, and Mrs. Dominic C. Armanino, former wife of, the late Dominic C. Armanino, author of several domino game instruction books; Shire Publications Ltd., UK, publisher of R.C. Bell's book, *Discovering Dice and Dominoes*. My thanks also go to the following domino manufacturers and distributors for all their wonderful help: Bonnie Tanner at Cardinal Industries; Bill Chiu and David Kessler at Plastech Industries; Hudson Dobson at Gamesource Limited; Lori Long at Creative Teaching Associates; and Charles T. Chiang of Domino32. A special thanks is in order to Scott Pitzer of Puremco Dominoes.

Index

Page numbers in *italics* indicate rules.

If you liked this book, you'll love all the titles in this series:

• Little Giant Book of After School Fun • Little Giant Book of Amazing Mazes • Little Giant Book of Brain Twisters • Little Giant Book of Card games • Little Giant Book of Card Tricks • Little Giant Book of Dominoes • Little Giant Book of Dinosaurs • Little Giant Book of Giggles • Little Giant Book of Jokes • Little Giant Book of Kids' Games • Little Giant Book of Knock-Knocks • Little Giant Book of Magic Tricks • Little Giant Book of Math Puzzles • Little Giant Book of Mini-Mysteries • Little Giant Book of Optical Illusions • Little Giant Book of Optical Tricks • Little Giant Book of Riddles • Little Giant Book of School Jokes • Little Giant Book of Science Experiments • Little Giant Book of Tongue Twisters • Little Giant Book of Travel Fun • Little Giant Book of Travel Games • Little Giant Book of "True" Ghostly Tales • Little Giant Book of "True" Ghost Stories • Little Giant Book of Visual Tricks • Little Giant Book of Whodunits

Available at fine stores everywhere.